LEADING A LIFE OF
IMPACT

LEADING A LIFE OF
IMPACT

DISCOVERING THE PATH
TO SELF-AWARENESS

LARRY EIDE

Two Harbors Press,
Minneapolis

Two Harbors Press
322 First Avenue N, 5th floor
Minneapolis, MN 55401
612.455.2293
www.TwoHarborsPress.com

ISBN-13: 978-1-62652-600-6
LCCN: 2013923369

Distributed by Itasca Books

Book Design by Mary Kristin Ross

Printed in the United States of America

WITH APPRECIATION

I want to extend special thanks to Janet Haag, Nancy Glatt, and Heather Eide for their assistance in the initial reviewing this manuscript. I am also grateful to Edwin Tsang and those who have aided him in the translation of the book into Chinese. Further, I express thanks to my wife, Diane, for her constant support and encouragement in our marriage and in a variety of leadership settings. Without it, the tremendous journey we've been on throughout thirty-eight years of marriage and vocation, and our excitement about the future, would never have been possible. Finally, I want to say how thankful I am to be a father to Heather, Amber, Angela, and Jarod. My relationship to each of them has been a very important part of learning to live and lead with growing joy and effectiveness.

ABOUT THE AUTHOR

Larry Eide grew up on the West Coast, largely in locations around Washington and Oregon. He received a Bachelor of Science degree from Seattle Pacific University, a Masters of Divinity from Canadian Theological Seminary (now Ambrose University), and a Doctorate from Trinity Western University, with a focus on leadership and spiritual formation. His lifetime of organizational leadership experiences in both the United States and Canada have given him an understanding of many of the struggles and challenges of leadership, as well as a commitment to being a supporting influence for leaders. He has been happily married for thirty-eight years to his wife, Diane, and they have four adult children, whom they deeply love and enjoy. He, therefore, also has experience leading a family, as well as within organizations.

For the past fifteen years, he has served as an assistant district superintendent for the Christian and Missionary Alliance denomination in British Columbia, Canada. He assists leaders and congregations in more than eighty churches, but he also works cooperatively and closely with leaders of a variety of denominations, as well as teams of leaders from across Canada.

Praise for *Leading a Life of Impact*

I have had the privilege of working closely with Larry Eide over the past decade. He is a leader with great sensitivity and insight. His passion has always been to help leaders have a better understanding of who they are in order to maximize and leverage their uniqueness. In his book, *Leading a Life of Impact*, Larry takes a well-researched and clearly relevant approach to opening the doors to the inner chambers of a leader. One of the most powerful challenges is around a leader's self-awareness. Knowing yourself, including your blind spots, is vital to effective and sustainable leadership. Larry has demonstrated that kind of leadership over the years. I highly recommend this book and believe it will serve as a significant tool in the leader's toolbox to empower sustainable and life-transforming impact.

—Reverend David Hearn, president of the Christian and Missionary Alliance in Canada

Successful leadership is not possible unless you know yourself. Larry's book takes you on a journey of self-discovery and self-awareness critical for anyone and everyone who desires to be an effective leader. There has never been a greater need for skilled and capable leaders than right now—and this book equips individuals in this quest.

—Ken Keis, MBA, president and CEO of Consulting Resource Group; author of *Why Aren't You More Like Me? Discover the Secrets to Understanding Yourself and Others*

I find this book so helpful because it helps me to know, to understand, and most importantly, to accept myself. In this postmodern twenty-first century, when people are given to individualism and self-egoism, it is necessary to refocus, re-examine, and know more about ourselves. This book provides a very good source for knowing ourselves so that we can serve better.

—Reverend Edwin Tsang, director of Chinese Ministries, Far East Broadcasting Associates of Canada

Larry stresses the importance of leading out of a keen sense of self-understanding. This book will equip you in your leadership role as you learn about yourself, how to deal with the challenges of leadership, and reaching your full potential, influencing those around you.

—Margaret Aubin, director of women's ministry, Saddleback Church, Rancho Capistrano campus

We need this tried and trusted information.

—Lorna Dueck, president and executive producer, *Context with Lorna Dueck* television show; journalist and media personality

As an entrepreneur who has built a substantial group of successful businesses that employ over 350 staff, the topic of leadership has, and continues to be, forefront in my mind as the key to my business success. Over the years I have attended many leadership seminars and read countless books on the subject of leadership. In my opinion, *Leading a Life of Impact* by Dr. Larry Eide encourages us to dig much deeper into the DNA of what successful leadership looks like from a Christian perspective. Larry's book brought a fresh perspective to me and without a doubt is helping me reshape my own leadership approach. I would highly recommend this book to everyone as a guide to developing your own personal leadership style. *Leading a Life of Impact* is a must read!

—Tom Watson, entrepreneur; international speaker; consultant; author of *Man Shoes*

CONTENTS

Preface : *Why this Book Is for You* xiii

Chapter 1: Know Your *Stage of Life* 1

Chapter 2: Know Your *Background* 13

Chapter 3: Know Your *Strengths* 21

Chapter 4: Know Your *Weaknesses* 29

Chapter 5: Know Your *Personality* 39

Chapter 6: Know Your *Temperament* 49

Chapter 7: Know Your *Passions* 57

Chapter 8: Know Your *Setting* 65

Chapter 9: Know Your *Spiritual Self* 75

Chapter 10: Know Your *Limits* 83

Chapter 11: Know Your *Family* 93

Chapter 12: Know Your *Body* 101

Chapter 13: Know Your *Mental Health* 109

Chapter 14: Know Your *Dream Scheme* 121

Chapter 15: Know Your *Blind Spots* 129

Epilogue 139

PREFACE: Why this Book Is for You

Why another book about gaining a better understanding of who you are? Don't most of us have a pretty good idea of what makes up the package that constitutes "me"? While we all would like to think so, our grasp of the person we think we are is at the worst delusional and at the best deficient. No one else lives in your skin or knows more about you than yourself, yet the complexity of who you are is like a jigsaw puzzle with a thousand pieces; and the more pieces that fit together, the more a picture begins to form. Beryl Markham, an aviatrix, made the alarming statement: "You can live a lifetime and, at the end of it, know more about other people than you know about yourself." While that may be true, it need not be true of you!

Two things need to be said about why this book is for you. First, you need to understand that you have a leadership influence on others, regardless of whether you are recognized as a leader by title or job description. I have been part of lively discussions where the topic is "What is a leader?" The only conclusion I ever came to in those discussions was that there are as many different definitions of leadership as there are participants in the discussion.

Few can seem to agree on a clear description. Perhaps that in itself is an indicator of the fact there are many different kinds of leaders who function within a diversity of settings, roles, and organizations. Some seem to be born leaders; others seem to be molded into leadership capabilities by the circumstances, opportunities, and testings that life affords them. Some who would never think of themselves as leaders find themselves in crisis situations or unique moments when they feel compelled to intervene and address the need.

Many would describe a stereotypical image of a leader to be the CEO of a company, a military officer, or an elected political official, and narrow their concept to those who give direction to a significant number of others. Still others would describe their image of a leader by referring to a dynamic encounter with an individual who significantly influenced them or impressed them with their skill in achieving specific results.

So really, what is a leader? Who can be called leaders? And what do leaders do?

As I have personally wrestled with those questions, it seems clear to me that at its basic foundation, leadership could be described as *moving others toward a desired outcome.* Whether that comes through the use of authority, personality, relational trust, skillful oratory, personal encouragement, or other means, leadership involves influencing others to move in specific directions or toward specific ends. In that sense, *anyone* who impacts or influences others toward a desired outcome could be considered a leader.

That's an uncommon way of looking at leadership, I know, but think about it. As a parent, don't you try to influence your children to become wholesome people, responsible citizens, and mature individuals? That's leadership! As a friend to others, don't you try to be a positive influence on them in order for them to enjoy that relationship and be influenced in healthy ways? That's leadership! As you voluntarily coach that sports team or team of people united by a common task, aren't you trying to achieve an outcome that in some way benefits your community? That's leadership! So is the effort of an individual to compile a list of signatures in order to express a concern or challenge the direction of a corporate entity or an elected official. You express leadership in many ways and at various times because, at its core, leadership is about influence and moving others toward a desired outcome. Therefore, this book is a helpful tool because it contains advice and information that applies to a multitude of leadership roles.

I am assuming in my previous statement that you desire to impact others in positive and powerful ways. The reason I say that is the difference between leadership (moving others toward a desired outcome) that positively impacts others and manipulation. Leadership, when used as it should be, will move others in directions that will be for their own good, as well as the good of others. Manipulation serves the selfish ego of those who would put themselves and their own desires above the good or desires of others. Although the latter moves others toward a designated outcome, and could be termed *negative* leadership or *deficit* leadership, it is vastly different from leadership that moves others toward positive outcomes, values, or goals that will produce benefit to themselves or others. Self-awareness is more than self-discovery by yourself, for yourself. It is not only for your own benefit but also for the benefit of others.

However you, like I, have an infinite capacity to fool yourself, and are limited in being able to see yourself completely objectively. So how can you know yourself honestly and realistically? Self-understanding largely comes through being in community and relating with others. It comes over a lifetime of experience and not in one quick shot. No author can lead you into complete and final understanding of the totality of who you are. However, in the pages that follow, I will suggest a number of factors that, while perhaps not exhaustive, are foundational and critical to you experiencing the ability to effectively, authentically, and powerfully impact others. You, like everyone, have the potential to impact and lead others, influencing them toward positive, helpful, or desirable outcomes, and that's why I have written this book for you.

The second reason why this book is for you is that many of you reading it will also be in formal, recognized positions of leadership, and a healthy self-awareness is critical to your ability to lead those in your community, organization, or team in healthy and productive ways. The power of self-awareness in leading others cannot be overly stated.

Bruce Gordon, in his book *Strategic Cheriths*, quotes the observation of a leadership consultant after working with a number of senior leaders from Fortune 500 companies: "Bruce, I am seeing absolute brilliance with minimal self-awareness."[1] What an amazing statement! Think of it! Leaders of Fortune 500 companies who are characterized by "absolute brilliance with minimal self-awareness." The implications on those leaders' lives and their leadership can be numerous yet also limiting, if not destructive. I say this because I've seen it happen in the lives of many leaders, and you probably have too.

What is true of Fortune 500 company executives can also be true of any leader. That's why I believe your ability to understand and accept who you are is an amazing gift. You'll never be the individual or the leader you could be without a healthy and increasing self-understanding. Further, without it, you'll never be able to effectively lead others because, until you gain a better understanding of yourself, you won't be able to better understand those you lead. Let me say again: when you better understand yourself, you can better understand and lead others!

---

1. Bruce E. Gordon, *Strategic Cheriths: God's Rest Areas*, (Bloomington: AuthorHouse, 2009), 49.

I have been in designated roles of leadership for most of my life, including organizational leadership for well over three decades, and am aware of the challenges, struggles, joys, pain, rewards, demands, insecurities, opportunities, and fulfillments that come in leading others toward positive outcomes and designated ends. On the other hand, I have seen many leaders struggle and lose not only hope, but health, family, jobs, confidence, and direction for a variety of reasons. For some, the disheartening experience within their leadership journey has reaped negative and lasting results. Others simply have given up the task too soon and changed their lives and careers, in the belief that perhaps their role in leadership was not the place or vocation in which they could best contribute.

Can you, as a leader, avoid the situations that could potentially destroy you? Can you carry out your role without crashing and burning and perhaps disappointing, or even destroying, others in the process? Can you experience longevity and health and influence others in ways that mutually make lives, communities, and organizations better? I believe you can.

One of the greatest challenges I have observed in others, though, during a lifetime of leadership roles, is the ability to know yourself and to lead out of a clear sense of who you are and are not. Along with this is knowing how this affects every decision and outcome in your life and leadership, as well as your organization, no matter how large or small it may be. I am convinced, from personal experience as well as my own doctoral studies in leadership, that one of the greatest assets you, as a leader, can have is the ability to lead out of a keen sense of self-understanding, to lead from within as an authentic extension of all you are. To know yourself is an incredible gift to your own life, as well as the lives of others.

Personally, it took me almost five decades to come to a place where I felt I truly knew myself and was satisfied "in my own skin." The totality of my life as a man, husband, father, friend, leader, and son is a picture in which the pieces are still forming and creating an image that may never be complete, no matter the length of my life. However, my understanding of all that I represent has never been clearer. This has enabled me to be comfortable with who I am, aiding me in making decisions for my life that have reflected that awareness. As a result, I have had greater freedom to live without longing to be something, or someone, else. I desire the same for you.

In writing this book, I have written out of a passion for you to succeed in accomplishing a successful life and vocation, and to finish both of these well. I have endeavored to write in a manner that extends beyond my own Christian vocation and in a way that will benefit any reader, whether or not you identify with my community of faith. You will, however, identify with the practical and helpful insights shared here, which will lead you toward a fuller understanding of who you uniquely are, and how that can affect the manner in which you live, as well as how you impact others.

Whether or not you lead others organizationally, may you find help and hope in these words. In whatever capacity you influence others, may you find in these chapters nuggets for your consideration and practice that will make your leadership stronger, more effective, more fulfilling to yourself, and more rewarding for those around you. You matter! How you lead matters! Whether you are a minister or other religious leader (like myself), a CEO, military officer, small business owner, parent, teacher, politician, job foreman, coach, neighborhood relational catalyzer, paid supervisor, or if you lead in another capacity, this book is dedicated to YOU. Each chapter is intended to help you become a more authentic, effective person and leader of others. As you read the pages ahead, realize more than ever what an amazing and unique individual you are. Learn to enjoy and appreciate your true self, not who you may wish you were, and let this guide you into a more rewarding, fulfilling, and effective future. Let the journey begin!

one

KNOW YOUR STAGE OF LIFE

"We can't become what we need to be by remaining what we are."
—Oprah Winfrey, media personality

Leadership Lesson

Each stage of life will play an immeasurable role in affecting your life and the impact your life has on others, making it vitally important that you understand the characteristics, challenges, and changes in each of those stages.

Each year for the past number of years, I have helped plan and lead retreats for others especially for the purposes of refreshment, networking, and connecting with peers. One of my favorite groups I've met with yearly has been young leaders, mostly in their twenties and thirties, making them roughly equal to my children's ages, but they have accepted me and treated me as one of their own. We have sometimes met at a beautiful location in southern British Columbia, using a gorgeous camp facility in the middle of a valley surrounded by forested hills. A lake fills the valley and makes the camp an ideal setting for a retreat.

One of the things these young leaders enjoyed in the evenings, after all our organized activities were over, was getting together on the ball hockey court, dividing into two teams, and having a friendly, though intense, competition. Since I did not grow up around hockey, I had never developed a passion for the game, nor had I ever played it, so I'd been quite content to watch and converse with those who came off the court as substitutes came on. However, on one particular night, they were pressuring me to play with them. I explained that I'd never played, knew nothing of the game, and would only be an embarrassment. But they continued to press, so finally, in a moment of weakness, in the name of camaraderie (or insanity, I'm not sure which), I said I'd give it a try.

Either their confidence was very high in my ability to learn or they wanted me out of the way, because the next thing I knew, they were strapping goalie pads on me, putting a mask over my head, a stick in my hand, and positioning me in front of a net. Me—a goalie? For the next two hours, I was like a bull's-eye on a rifle range, and I took hit after hit after hit. My team lost, but I must have done a few things right because they raved about some of the saves I made, apparently a good showing for a first-time target. I thanked them and tried to act like it was really nothing, but the black and blue marks all over my body (the pads only partly covered me) said otherwise. If it was nothing, how come I hurt so much?

The experience wasn't complete, however, because the very next night they drafted me again. Not wanting to disappoint them, and not wanting to tell my ego to act my age, I said yes, once again becoming a human target. After a second night of "taking it for the team," and being the last night of the retreat, I decided that next year I would find ways to connect with them that were more in keeping with who I am, instead of who I'm not. And so I retired my jersey (actually, I didn't have a jersey, but that's hockey talk for hanging up the skates).

You, like I, have had experiences when you wanted to make a favorable impression on others, prove something to yourself, or haven't wanted to admit the limitations of your age, resulting in your acting in ways that have at best worked out or at worst landed you in an emergency ward. Perhaps you've spent large amounts of time and money buying and using products that camouflage your age, or engaging in athletic activities to convince yourself you're younger than you actually are. Perhaps as a child you couldn't wait to grow up, but are finding as an adult that you want to be a kid again.

If you are raising a family, you know you have to make sacrifices, but sometimes you may find yourself fighting the notion of giving up some of what you enjoyed in the past in order to devote yourself to your present reality. If you've moved into your middle years, you may be experiencing hormonal changes and sometimes end up doing unusual, irrational, or uncharacteristic things as you experience bodily and emotional changes that you would rather deny. Perhaps, like myself, you have been playfully, or seriously, accused of a midlife crisis simply because you've purchased something you couldn't afford earlier in life, like my convertible, which is fairly old but not a bad-looking car. However, as you look around and see many middle-aged individuals riding motorcycles or buying convertibles or other expensive "toys," don't you sometimes wonder how many are a reflection of a battle to turn back the pages of time?

You're in the company of multitudes if you have moments when you wish you could turn back time and relive an experience or an era that was meaningful or enjoyable for you. How often do you hear a song that was popular in your teenage or young adult years and it makes you flash back in your memories and wish you could experience some of those special moments again?

One of the hit songs by a group of yesteryear, The Byrds, based on Ecclesiastes 3 from the Bible, echoed these words: *"To everything (Turn, Turn, Turn) / There is a season (Turn, Turn, Turn) / And a time to every purpose, under Heaven."* For all of us, life is a series of seasons, of ages, stages, and gauges that mark the progression from childhood to adolescence to youth to adulthood. Each of these stages of life has certain experiences that are common, though not all experiences are universal. As mortal humans, some of the characteristics and experiences of these stages can be altered but not completely eliminated. For example, you may eat a healthy diet, exercise regularly, work at getting rest, and try to live a balanced lifestyle so that you can move into the next stage of life healthy, flexible, and as mentally sharp as possible.

Nonetheless, you may have to admit that for all you do, you simply do not have the energy and capacity that you had a decade or two ago. I know in my own case, I look back at the decades of my twenties, thirties, forties, and fifties and can see differences in the way I have felt, thought, and viewed myself and life around me. Many of those differences are not a matter of right or wrong, but simply reflect differences that came from growing older and maturing, and having more of life's experiences to draw on. If there is anything you can count on in the years, it's the guarantee of changes and challenges that are age and stage specific.

As I am writing largely to an adult audience, allow me to suggest that your adulthood will be comprised of four stages. Many authors have attempted to articulate various life stages, but I am suggesting four descriptors for adulthood in which there is some measure of overlap and will not perfectly describe the experience of every human being. However, they will at least expose a general commonality. With these descriptors, I will offer a few thoughts on what characterizes each and some of the key motivators involved. I would describe those four stages as:

1. **Making a place** (20s–30s): the struggle of moving from youth to adulthood
2. **Making an identity** (30s–40s): adults struggling with realities of adulthood
3. **Making a difference** (40s–50s): adults struggling with the meaning of adulthood
4. **Making a legacy** (50s–60s+): adults struggling to be youthful again and how to leave an imprint

As you move into your twenties and thirties and are engaged in "making a place" in the world for yourself, you may find yourself at the end of your formal education and now beginning to pay back a significant debt incurred by that experience. In this stage you look for work, possibly start a career, and seek to rent or buy a living space you can call your own. Such goals can begin a new cycle of debt. Your first job may become the first of a string of jobs as you provide for your needs but also seek to find your fit.

In this stage, you find (or should find) many attitudes you held in your teen years are changing, and you desire to establish independence from the past financial support of your parents. You begin taking more responsibility for yourself, while establishing a few core friendships that will hopefully help carry you through this stage and perhaps last the rest of your life. This stage can be characterized by a struggle for security, a need for a sense of belonging, for stability, and a drive to experience life to its fullest. It can also be a rude awakening, a reality check. However, these experiences, too, can contribute to your growth, and to your ability to make good decisions.

Some of the key motivators in this stage can be a thirst for adventure, a need to "find yourself," general restlessness, insecurity, a need for relationships, a desire to "grow up," and either a genuine concern or lack of concern about the future.

Gordon MacDonald, in his book *A Resilient Life*[1], expresses these stages a little differently, but he is helpful in articulating some of the key questions that characterize each stage. For example, questions in your twenties and thirties revolve around:

- The kind of person you're becoming
- How to make meaningful and enduring friendships
- What to do with your life
- What core beliefs or values you will center your life around
- How to prioritize the many demands of life
- How to pay the bills
- Whether your life is on track with desirable goals
- How to counter loneliness and relational needs (especially males)
- How to continue growing into the person you would like to be

For many in this stage, there is also a strong sense of social concern already developed, or in the process of developing, which needs expression. This desire to make a difference in others' lives is a prime example of the fact that the descriptors I use for each stage are not confined to those stages, but are generally true.

Moving through your thirties and into your forties, some of those questions and motivators continue, but others are added to them. In this stage, as you seek to solidify an identity, you may be

---

1. Gordon MacDonald, *A Resilient Life* (Nashville: Nelson Books, 2004), 52–58.

identifying with a particular vocation and are working to excel, or even advance, in that vocation. It may not be a job you desire, but a career. If it hasn't already happened, you may be seeking someone to share life with and build a family. Time and energy are in high demand for you, and you may find the need to sacrifice a few things or choose between things you were dreaming about for the future, or you may need to put those dreams on hold while you attend to more immediate priorities. Raising families and/or your vocation can often seem all consuming. You may be driven by great expectations, or limited by less-than-ideal realities.

Some of the key motivators in this stage can be survival, changing priorities, building a future, earning power, and even idealism about what you want from life. To some of those questions already mentioned, MacDonald adds questions about the complexities of life and a growing awareness of your limitations, including, perhaps, struggles with where you're at in life in comparison to others. As you change physically, and your family and needs change, questions arise about your goals, or you struggle with current realities. Uncertainties about the future and the sense of the lost past can be unsettling. It can be, however, a strategic time to wrestle with such questions and rechart or reconfirm a course for the future.

Your forties and fifties become a time of trying to move beyond those questions into more certainty about the future and desiring to find more meaning to your life, such as how to make a real difference in the world and not just "a living." This can potentially lead to a career change, or at least to a search for how you can make a difference beyond the confines of your employment situation. This can potentially lead to real soul searching, even a crisis of experience. Added to this, changes in your physical, emotional, and mental being may lead to a midlife crisis.

A growing sense of your mortality can hit you squarely and collide with some of your motivations.

Perhaps those motivations come from a maturity you learned through the experiences of life, or struggles with life's realities, or a heightened social conscience. You may think more about "the bigger picture," leading you to feel affirmed in your direction or to see life as having largely passed you by. This stage can be characterized by idealism colliding with realities, the effects of the onslaught of aging, hormonal imbalances, or even a driving need for further growth, learning, or retooling.

In the midst of these experiences and challenges, questions may stir you, such as:

- What may have produced certain results in some of your relationships
- Whether your life will have many more years
- Why some of those close to you have died or taken destructive pathways
- Why time seems to move so quickly
- How to deal with dramatic physical or inward changes
- How to prepare adequately for the "retirement" phase
- How to deal with nagging fears and personal doubts

As you move from the fifties into the sixties and beyond, the desire to make a difference becomes even more acute and can become a quest to leave a legacy in life. You look at ways this could happen. You desire to leave a lasting and positive imprint in your family, your community, and your organization, if not your larger world. In this stage, the mentored become the mentors, at least in a more intentional sense, while also recognizing the need for ongoing learning and growth in your own life. At the same time, the experiences and learning of life find need for expression. Relationally, you may be adjusting to the reality of being an "empty nester" with your children no longer living at home, or you may be facing the reality of living alone after the death of a spouse or following a divorce. You give even more thought to the realities and needs of retirement and continued aging. As a result, you may be stepping up efforts at healthy diets, regular exercise, and financial enhancement.

You wrestle with a series of choices that will influence how you live and how you will finish in the remainder of your life. The growing sense of social consciousness, which has been present before, may now be complementary to this stage of life when you can afford the time or resources to pursue it more fully. Your life may be characterized by the big picture realization of the brevity of life, and either a tendency to be self-serving or to serve others so they can benefit from your learning, resources, or abilities. Quality relationships become even more important to you, and you may have fewer, but better, friendships.

Some of the key motivators for this phase can be:

- A desire for immortality
- A desire to leave the world a better place
- A genuine concern for the needs of others
- Loneliness, panic, or concern over the future
- Struggles with changing realities that significantly impact you

Change is natural throughout life, but you may struggle with change more than ever. As a result of these realities, questions can arise about feeling sidelined, ignored, or unappreciated. Questions can revolve around what you have accomplished or can yet accomplish in what time is left, or about the impact of death on you or your family if your spouse dies, or about unrealized dreams. Core convictions, or the ability of these to carry you forward, may come into question. Questions can also arise concerning what your accomplishments have meant, how you can continue leaving an imprint, the impact of things you can or cannot control, why certain emotions seem so intense, and the meaning of life or life after death.

You may describe the stages of life and adulthood somewhat differently. You may recognize certain characteristics, questions, or experiences that have affected you differently in the timeline of your own life. What's critical to recognize is that as life evolves, there will be experiences that are unique to each of us, yet also experiences common to us all. These experiences will play a powerful role in the development of the person you become and how you influence others around you.

For Individual Consideration or Group Discussion

Which of the four stages of life mentioned would best describe your own current experience? What words would you use to describe motivators and characteristics in your stage of life? List as many as you can, and beside each one write "strongly influences me," "somewhat influences me," or "does not influence me."

Example: Making a Difference (40s–50s)

• Lost my job, seeking a second career	strongly influences me
• Parent died last year	strongly influences me
• Hormonal changes, moody	somewhat influences me
• Moved to a new home	does not influence me
• Coaching boys basketball team	strongly influences me

Which of these life influencers would you consider unique to yourself or common to people in general?

Example:

- Coaching community basketball team   unique to my own situation
- Moved to a new home   common experience

As you consider those descriptors for your stage of life, which ones do you need to give special attention to? Might you need the help of others in processing your experience, ensuring that it is formative instead of detrimental to your life and impact on others?

Example:

- Parent died last year $\rightarrow$ Still overwhelmed by grief; may need to see a counselor or clergy.
- Lost my job, seeking career $\rightarrow$ May need retooling. See a job counselor to explore career path options or training available online or by local schools or organizations.
- Struggle with mood swings $\rightarrow$ See a doctor regarding possible hormonal changes, stress factors, physical changes, or other factors.

What are some of the potential realities of your next stage of life, and are there ways you can begin preparing even now to address them?

Example: Making a Legacy (50s–60s+)

- Vocational changes   educational training
- Empty nester   take up a hobby with my spouse
- Health issues due to aging develop a program of regular exercise

ACTION STEPS

1. Read magazines or books, or access other resources, describing characteristics of your current (or next) stage of life and consider ways to live and work at your optimum.

Example:

- Helpful authors on raising a family
- Webinars on financial planning
- Resources discussing how to lead a team

2. Seek the help of professionals, or people more capable than yourself, who can help address specific areas of concern.

Example:

- Retirement planner
- Medical doctor
- Marriage counselor
- Debt counselor
- Job counselor

two

KNOW YOUR BACKGROUND

"Self-knowledge is the beginning of self-improvement."
—Spanish proverb

Leadership Lesson

Be aware that who you are and how you lead others has been influenced by your past, for better or worse. Draw on those aspects of your past that have shaped you positively and deal with tendencies that tend to sabotage your efforts by first asking yourself why you have that tendency, how it is affecting your life and leadership, and what might need changing.

Imagine the following, which although fictional, personifies the experience of many of us to different degrees. It involves "Mark," who had started out in his company in a low-paying support role, but liked the company and saw potential for a real future with it. His hard work and good ideas were being rewarded. Although he had only been with them for a couple of years, he was given a managerial role in which he supervised eight others. At first the challenge was exciting, though it drew on all his abilities and often left him exhausted at the end of the day. He found both his abilities and his inexperience confirmed and made a decision early on that he should focus on what played to his strengths, but would hope others on his team would care for those things that underscored his inexperience. Avoidance of those difficult things quickly became a pattern, but instead of others picking up on them and covering for his inattention to these challenges, it began to eat away at the other members of his team. Relational tensions developed between Mark and his coworkers; mistrust, complaints, and criticisms became standard fare.

After a few months of mounting tensions and dysfunctional efforts in working through several short-term projects, which just could not seem to gel under Mark's leadership, and his self-admitted inability to discern the source of the problem, he called a team meeting to discuss the situation. He invited open and honest discussion, assuring his coworkers their comments would be taken seriously and kept confidential. Much to his surprise, having suspected the problem was his team, the discussion revealed patterns of avoidance on Mark's part. Certain things got his attention, but other things, sometimes important things, were given little focus. Due to time sensitivity in some instances, deadlines and opportunities had been missed.

As Mark was confronted with his tendency to avoid difficult tasks due to his inexperience and insecurities, he began contemplating his patterns. Why did he tend to avoid rather than confront such difficulties? He desired to be an effective leader, but he found his inattention to certain tasks was instead producing a deteriorating work environment for his team. Where did this tendency come from? What circumstances tended to trigger an attitude of avoidance when faced with situations in which he was unfamiliar and untrained? Could it be the result of negative past experiences? Or even the example of his own father, whom he realized used to respond in the same manner when relating to his family and others? It became clear that understanding his past might unlock a pathway to a more effective future as a leader at work and with his family. He decided to seek out a counselor who could help him clarify his struggles and their root causes, connecting his past experience to his current realities.

This fictional scenario has probably played itself out in some way in your own life. You may not have even realized it. You may have experienced struggles with your coworkers, as Mark did, or perhaps difficulties arose within your marriage, which you may or may not have realized had roots in your background. Perhaps the struggles weren't relational but were internal, leading you to depression, discouragement, and to personal choices that were less than desirable and made you wish you could go back and do things differently. It may be that you've wondered why you respond in certain ways to a specific person or to specific circumstances. More than likely, the answer is rooted in your background experiences.

There was a period of my career when I traveled around North America a great deal, spending a majority of the year in towns and cities other than the one where I lived, which at that time was Minneapolis. This was before global positioning devices were implanted in our cell phones, telling us when to turn and leading us with ease into strange places. I now enjoy simply plugging in an address and letting my GPS take me where I want to go. However, in those days when I traveled heavily, I had to depend on local maps, the bystanders' directions, and a fair amount of common sense to help me reach my destinations, especially when journeying around unfamiliar cities. Admittedly, I allowed my "male qualities" to convince me at times that I did not need to ask for directions and could find my way with simple deductive reasoning and a little luck.

All too often, however, I'd find myself lost and I would have to humbly ask for assistance. I have related to a number of people over the years that I've learned my way around more cities by getting lost!

What do my own directional dysfunctions have to do with you? The idea of knowing where you are in relation to where you've been and where you want to go has great relevance to the ability to know yourself. You are a product of your past. You are who you are in part because of your unique personality and inner qualities. Yet even your personality and inner qualities, along with your other traits, have been greatly influenced by your past experiences.

If you were asked to describe yourself to another person, you might begin by stating a few of your physical qualities, such as your height, age, hair color, weight, or the color of your eyes. You might tell me your cultural or racial background, perhaps as an Irish American, Native American, French Canadian, Chinese, or European. Perhaps you would describe yourself in terms of hobbies, such as being an avid reader, tennis player, or golfer. You might even describe your likes and dislikes, your state of health, or your vocation.

All of these could be said to describe, in part, what makes up the person you are. However, it might not be your first inclination to describe yourself in terms of your past. For instance, in my own case, my first inclination might not be to tell others that I grew up in a small town in Oregon (population 1,200) and that I attended a high school of fewer than two hundred students, which gave me opportunity to be involved in a number of activities, such as school sports and student government. Or I might not mention that for years as a young boy I used to work in my father's small town pharmacy, cleaning its floors, tidying its shelves, and assisting customers. I might fail to mention that I am the oldest of four siblings (three brothers and a sister) and that the sense of family was strong in our household. It might not be my first tendency to tell you that I grew up in the Presbyterian Church in that small town, so to some degree faith was an integral part of my life from the time I was young. When I graduated from high school, I left that small town for a large city, moving to Seattle to enter university, where I spent the next four years involved in academic, leadership, and social activities that were formative. Following graduation, I traveled around the Central and Eastern United States for a year, which is how I met my wife. I have lived and worked in diverse places. I have raised four children. All of these things had a shaping influence on my life. Not only the good and desirable things, but also those things that have been difficult and painful. All of them have influenced me and molded me into the person I am today.

The same is true of you, and those you impact. No matter how or where you were raised, whether it was in a city or on a farm, no matter what kind of family you came from, or the kind of education you had, it all has left a mark on your life. Perhaps that includes some dysfunctional and undesirable aspects to your family life or life experience, but these, too, have had a formative impact on you. Some of the effects of your past may need to be faced and overcome, and that is also a shaping experience.

However, the bottom line is that who you are today has been influenced by your past. It is equally true that who you will become tomorrow will be greatly influenced by how you live and the choices you make today. Therefore, the importance of understanding yourself in light of your background experience cannot be overstated.

One of the greatest influences of your past was your family of origin. You may have had close family relationships, open communication, respect, and appreciation; or you may have had broken relationships, abuse, and dysfunctional or nonexistent communication with your parents or siblings. Patterns of thinking and acting begin to form very early in life. Various sources suggest the first five years of one's life as the most formative. Even so, the experiences of teen years, young adulthood, the early years of marriage or beginning a career, and every stage of life up to the present have played a part in shaping you. Many have instilled positive qualities, good values, and helpful abilities. Still others have influenced you in ways that you may not even be aware of.

How did your family handle conflict? What subjects were openly discussed and which were taboo? What was the leadership style of your father and mother? How did they handle difficulties? How did members of your family relate to one another? Was your family influenced by strong traditions or cultural realities? Was your family good at expressing appreciation, affirming others, or functioning as a unit? How were anger and negative emotions expressed or viewed in your family? What do you recall as being some of your best and worst experiences early in life, and what made them so?

How would you describe your experiences in the first jobs you held? What made them good or difficult experiences? What are some of your first recollections of feeling good about yourself and what stirred those feelings?

What were the experiences you had in beginning to relate to the members of the opposite sex, and were those pleasant or unpleasant? What's the first major crisis in your life you can recall and what made it so?

The list of questions could continue building, but these illustrate how helpful, and revealing, it can be to reflect on your past in order to gain insight into your present experience. Know yourself! Know where you've come from and the influences that have shaped you.

For Individual Consideration or Group Discussion

What are experiences you can identify from your past that may have shaped you in positive ways, and how?

Example:

- I held jobs while attending school → taught me to discipline my time
- My parents had a good marriage → taught me how spouses relate in healthy ways

- Traveled a lot as a family → gave me a desire to experience other cultures
- Grew up in a large family → helped me learn how to relate to others
- Played team sports → taught me how to function with others as a team

Identify ways you are specifically struggling in your life or leadership, and list how those could potentially be a product of past influences.

Example:

- Struggling with my supervisor → I have always struggled with others in authority over me due to some bad experiences with authority figures
- My marriage is struggling → could be influenced by the difficult marriage my parents had, so I lacked a good model
- Restless in my job → could be influenced by my pattern of not committing to long-term situations or a tendency at times to move on when the going gets tough
- I'm reluctant to make tough decisions → I've struggled in the past with self-image and, therefore, want to be a people pleaser

ACTION STEPS

List ways you could potentially address your life and leadership struggles in positive ways.

Example:

- Try to see things through the eyes of my supervisor
- Work at being a model team member
- Talk to a friend who has a good marriage
- Seek out a good marriage or family counselor
- Read books on marriage and family relationships
- Recommit myself to the job or role I am in and set fresh, dynamic goals
- Make decisions based on the bigger picture and not just my personal situation
- Keep reminding myself that tough decisions are part of being a good leader
- Seek out a personal coach to help me address needed areas of development

three

KNOW YOUR STRENGTHS

"I believe that the measure of a person's life
is the effect they have on others."
—Steve Nash, NBA All-Star

Leadership Lesson

Each person has qualities and abilities that represent strengths, which when used will lead to more rewarding outcomes in their own life and the lives of others.

The idea of knowing your strengths may seem obvious and so basic that you are tempted to skip to the next chapter, thinking you already know yourself well. But wait! Do you *really* know your strengths? To what degree are you aware of them? Perhaps the most appropriate question is: How often do you regularly use those strengths in a setting that is a good fit for them?

The answer to those questions may not be as obvious as you think. Many of those who lead others are either unaware of their greatest strengths or are not empowered to use those strengths in a consistent way. It's also easy to become so absorbed in the demands of the immediate context that you become more focused on meeting those daily demands than on having your optimum effect. But you want more than this, don't you? You want to believe that your life and work are making a positive difference in the lives of others. The sobering and challenging truth is that your life is affecting others around you in unseen and profound ways. The effect you have on their lives will have results not only in the present but the future. The same could be said in terms of the impact of your leadership role. The present, as well as the future, will be impacted by the manner in which you lead others, and whether you have capitalized on your strengths to their (and your) advantage.

Understanding who you are, and accepting who you are, can be two parallel journeys that may not ever merge. My own past experience led me to believe that leadership in some way was going to be a significant part of my life, whether personally or professionally. Call it pride or ego, but for most of those years, I inwardly preferred to be in roles acknowledging me as the lead person, as opposed to being an associate or assistant. Over time I have experienced both, and found myself able to function in each role. Given my preference, I would have chosen to be "the leader." However, over the years I have come to understand that what's most important is to be functioning out of your strengths, whether or not you are the leader in charge.

North American society tends to place greater value on being the person in charge, but the fact of the matter is that the person in charge will never be an effective leader unless they not only are operating out of a sense of their own strengths, but have others around them who also are drawing on their own areas of strength. In recent years I have come to realize, and accept, that while I have served in chief and associate roles, my greatest impact in job settings has occurred when I have assisted "the leader." This is largely because my greatest strength is the ability to function as more of a generalist than as a specialist. I'm able to function effectively within a broader job description than in a narrowly focused role, which may be dependent on one specialty talent. This may or may not seem profound to those of you who are talented specialists, but to those who are generalists by nature, it can breathe life into what you do! It can bring renewed motivation, greater purpose, and energy.

Knowing your strengths not only makes you more effective, but it can generate the same results in others. As a leader, you may be focused on raising a family, leading a corporation, managing a small business, directing a sales team, or in some other way you may have responsibilities that entail influencing, if not outright directing, other people toward specific and desirable ends. However, and in whatever form you are endeavouring to influence others (and make the world a better place for them and yourself), a critical part of achieving that will be recognizing your strengths. Not only recognizing them, but making sure you are regularly drawing upon those strengths in your interactions with those around you.

You are a unique individual! There is no one else in this world exactly like you. You may bear similarities to others and have certain qualities or characteristics in common. You might even be what others call an "identical twin." However, in reality, you and you alone bear all the qualities and characteristics that make you the person you are. If you struggle with accepting yourself as you are, begin to regularly reflect on the qualities that make you unique and special, most especially the special talents you may possess, abilities that are not common to everyone else. Certain abilities and talents describe each one of us. Some of them you were naturally born with, others have developed through your life experiences, and depending on your belief system, some abilities are "God-given." This is true of every person, and it is true of you!

You may or may not be in a setting that allows those strengths to be used and to flourish. One of the important questions for any person to ask themself is whether they are being motivated by, and enabled to, freely use those abilities and talents that represent their strengths. If so, chances are you are experiencing a significant amount of fruitfulness and fulfillment in your setting. If you are not focusing on those strengths, you are probably experiencing a significant amount of conflict (inner as well as with others) or perhaps frustration and a lack of motivation. The latter experience is only natural when you are not living and leading out of the core of your inner person and your personal strengths. This can make a tremendous difference in whether you are simply living out of routine and leading as a duty, or you are finding life and energy in those daily routines and in your leadership of others.

Do you have a clear picture of what your strengths are and what abilities you seem drawn to use? If you think about settings or experiences where you have seen results that have positively influenced others and have given you an inner sense of real satisfaction, you will find examples of strengths that were put into practice. It is simply not true that there is nothing special or unique about you or that you do not have anything special to offer. You have strengths that can be used in constructive ways to bring positive results into the lives of others. In doing so, you will find personal joy and fulfillment. You will find yourself energized and motivated because you are operating out of a clear sense of the strengths that characterize your life. To borrow a golfer's term, you will find yourself in your "sweet spot."

On the other hand, you may not find yourself in a setting that calls on those strengths or allows for their regular expression. Are there ways you can incorporate those strengths into some of your duties, even if your job description does not call for them? Go beyond your job description, or look for an opportunity to step into a new role that matches your strengths. Perhaps there are ways in which you can put those strengths into practice outside your job role, such as meeting a need in your community or volunteering some of your time in activities that call upon your strengths. Use those strengths in addressing the needs and desires of your family.

Whatever your setting may be, and wherever you carry out your daily life and work, look for ways to match your strengths to the needs and challenges around you. If you do, you will find your greatest effectiveness in impacting others, and as a result, your greatest sense of personal satisfaction. The challenges that have created the greatest struggles for you and those around you will be met with greater confidence and will produce greater results because you have faced them by drawing on those qualities and abilities which most profoundly express the person you are!

For Individual Consideration or Group Discussion

List your personal characteristics that you would clearly identify as your personal strengths. This could include abilities or character qualities.

Example: personal abilities

- Relational, interact comfortably with diverse kinds of people
- Good administrator
- Musically skilled
- Love to work with numbers and complex budgets
- People respond well to me as a speaker
- Analyze problems and calculate solutions well
- Can see the big picture when others can't

Example: personal characteristics

- Calm under stressful circumstances
- Honest and dependable; people trust me
- Not easily discouraged, tenacious
- Strong work ethic
- Passionate about the needs of the poor
- Intuitive
- Unafraid to take risks after considering the costs

1.

2.

3.

4.

5.

Can you think of comments multiple people have made that could potentially identify other areas of strength you haven't listed above?

Example:

- Several people have commented on how effectively I organized events.
- When I have offered financial advice to others, I have had a number of them say how helpful that advice has been.
- Others have commented about the wisdom I bring into decision-making processes.

- Several people have expressed how helpful my counsel has been to them.
- My team has often commented on how I have influenced their ability to function as a unit.

In what kinds of situations have you seemed to be at your best?

Example:

- I seem to really do well at coaching sports teams with high school-aged people.
- I am happiest when I am helping another person who is in need.
- When others seem to get frustrated at problems, I seem to be able to see solutions.
- I particularly enjoy working with senior citizens.
- I think continually about how to help unemployed people find jobs.

ACTION STEPS

List ways to explore or to grow those strengths or special abilities you have identified.

Example:

- Get involved in an organization or community group focused on that interest.
- Read materials and books focused on identifying or developing those special abilities or interests. A simple word search of "identifying your strengths" on the web will reap many possible sources.
- Volunteer to assist a coach with a local sports team.
- Get involved in a local food bank.
- Take courses focused on leadership themes or furthering your counseling skills.
- Offer to serve on the organizing team for a special event at work or in your community.
- Participate in a personal strengths assessment via an online source, a jobs counselor, or your own organization's human resource department.

four

KNOW YOUR WEAKNESSES

". . . Leaders are people who are able to express themselves fully .
. . they know who they are, what their strengths and weaknesses
are, and how to fully deploy their strengths and compensate for
their weaknesses."
—Warren Bennis, On Becoming a Leader

Leadership Lesson

Weaknesses that cause you to act in ways that are unhealthy need to be acknowledged and addressed. However, recognizing and avoiding, or compensating for, personal weaknesses that simply reflect your inabilities or inexperience can make you stronger and a better leader.

The previous chapter focused on the necessity of understanding your strengths. Equally important is understanding your weaknesses. In some ways, knowing your weaknesses may even be more critical than knowing your strengths because it will not be your strengths that sabotage your dreams, damage relationships, short circuit your hard work, or prevent you from achieving your potential. It will be your weaknesses! Only when you understand your weaknesses can you find ways to improve them or be alert to the signals that something self-destructive is about to happen. When you understand them, you can avoid, or at least minimize, circumstances that tend to draw out those weaknesses like a giant magnet.

It's been a lesson in leadership over the years for me to observe others who seemed destined for great things but ended up with unrealized dreams and unfulfilled lives because they either spent their time working in a role that did not play to their strengths or they allowed their weaknesses to prematurely end their efforts to be successful. Some who seemed to be shooting stars quickly flamed out when they gave in to character weaknesses or made choices to act or lead in ways that violated the values of their organization, their own moral values, or those of others around them. Personal flaws or shortcomings can quickly bring a career, a life, a family, and untold potential crashing down around the person who ignores (or fails to calculate) the impact of their actions.

All of us have weaknesses, and those weaknesses come in many forms. They may simply be abilities or qualities that do not characterize you to the degree you see them in others. If so, these shortcomings are nothing to be ashamed of. I am not a skillful painter, nor do I have the singing voice of a professional musician or the specialized ability to take a failing organization and turn it into a winner. In fact, I'm not even very good at times at finding my car in a mall parking lot!

On the other hand, there are things I can do adequately or even very well. But for every thing I'm good at, there are at least twenty that I'm not! That's all right. No one can be good at everything. Accept that reality. It is only human when listening to an amazing singer to wish you had a voice like that, or to admire the skill of a professional athlete, or to wish you had the body of that person on the cover of the magazine in front of you at the supermarket checkout stand. Who hasn't fantasized about being a famous person in sports or entertainment, perhaps a rock star?

You have certain abilities, which represent strengths or special gifts, that you need to use. You also could name activities or tasks for which you need to depend on the strengths of others. That's okay. You can surround yourself with others who excel where you lack and whose capabilities can be a complement to your own. This makes a strong and dynamic team! No one is perfect, no one can do everything, and every one of us has aspects of our life we might like to improve upon. It's when you try to live someone else's reality, trying to be what you're not, and live dissatisfied because you are not like someone else or do not have the same strengths as another person that you miss the joys of appreciating your own strengths. Not only that, but you can become focused on abilities that may never be part of your reality, instead of enjoying those that are and improving those qualities or abilities that you can.

Some weaknesses relate to character inadequacies, personality flaws, destructive ways of thinking, or acting out your emotions, which you have picked up through bad experiences or bad mentors. They may be weaknesses related to personal immaturities or the actions of others toward you that deeply affected you. Such weaknesses may or may not in themselves be "wrong," but they can lead you to express yourself in destructive or counterproductive ways. Weaknesses such as these, when allowed to surface, can manifest themselves through hurtful words, foolish actions, impulsive decisions, and in other damaging ways. This can especially be true when the root of your action lies in a deep emotional or psychological pain arising from one or more past experiences.

A classic example is the person who was verbally or otherwise abused by others over time and, as a result, has become one who mirrors that in relation to others. Those who come from homes where addictions dominated (such as alcoholism or pornography) often find themselves struggling with the same issues. Those who have grown up in environments where lying or dishonesty was prevalent may find themselves acting similarly and may find integrity a constant challenge. When weaknesses like these are present in your life, you need to recognize them and receive help in overcoming them, or you will find them a constant stumbling block to yourself and others. That help can potentially come from a variety of sources who have the ability or training to help you see yourself more objectively and honestly than you can sometimes do on your own: a trusted pastor or priest, a professional counsellor or psychologist, a wise and able friend, a spouse who is able to be helpful without being hurtful.

A few years ago, I was part of a conference that met on a beautiful monastery campus that housed an order of Benedictine monks. On the wall of the building where we met and slept was a framed rule of Saint Benedict, which I felt compelled to photograph, especially for its last phrase. The ancient rule stated:

> If any pilgrim monk come from distant parts, if with wish as a guest to dwell in the monastery, and will be content with the customs which he finds in the place, and do not perchance by his lavishness disturb the monastery, but is simply content with what he finds, he shall be received, for as long a time as he desires. If, indeed, he find fault with anything, or expose it, reasonably, and with the humility of charity, the Abbott shall discuss it prudently, lest perchance God had

sent him for this very thing. But, if he have been found gossipy and contumacious in the time of his sojourn as guest, not only ought he not to be joined to the body of the monastery, but also it shall be said to him, honestly, that he must depart. **If he does not go, let two stout monks, in the name of God, explain the matter to him**.

What a great way of saying "let two stout bouncers throw him out on his ear!" How easy it is to recognize the weaknesses in others, but not always in yourself. And sometimes it takes someone, or something, acting as "two stout monks" to get your attention and make you aware that something about you needs to be thrown out on its ear.

Do you know your weaknesses? Are you able to admit and accept that you don't have a strength or ability you see in someone else, but which you admire? Are you developing a growing awareness of your personal qualities or characteristics that could potentially be self-sabotaging if left unchecked? Further, as a leader, are you growing in your awareness of the weaknesses of those around you that you may need to compensate for by drawing on the strengths of others, or which you or others may need to address?

A final word on knowing your weaknesses as well as your strengths: Have you ever heard it said "your greatest strengths can also be your greatest weaknesses"? While the statement may seem a contradiction, it's truer than you think. The very strengths that characterize you, if carried to extremes, can become counterproductive weaknesses. For example, your greatest strength may be the ability to look at a situation and assess it quickly and thoroughly. However, your ability to assess can become a weakness if it leads you to overanalyze situations to the point of indecision. Or perhaps you have a strength in being able to articulate your thoughts in clear and honest ways. That's good, unless you fail to also exercise discernment, timing, and tact in what you say. Speaking a thought without considering the potential impact, or speaking it to the wrong person or at the wrong time, can be disastrous and detrimental to your intended outcome.

Knowing both your strengths and your weaknesses, and how these can be personal manifestations of the same things, is an invaluable help in relating to others and leading them toward desirable results.

For Individual Consideration or Group Discussion

What would you identify as your personal weaknesses? Do these characterize a lack of ability or inexperience or a personal issue?

Example:

- Not very good at public speaking → lack of experience
- Not good at working with children → lack of ability
- Impatient → personal issue
- Always late for appointments → personal issue
- Don't meet strangers well → personal issue
- Don't work well under pressure → personal issue (or lack of ability?)
- Not a strong leader of groups → lack of experience

1.

2.

3.

4.

5.

Can you think of examples of situations that became negative experiences for you and what personal factors may have contributed to that, whether it was a personal issue, lack of experience, or lack of ability?

Example:

- Tried to correct person at work, backfired → wasn't tactful or patient
- Made suggestion to spouse of a problem → picked bad time, insensitive to her
- Made inappropriate joke, embarrassed → sometimes I crave attention
- Big fight with fellow team member → I can tend to insist on my own way

1.

2.

3.

4.

5.

Can you think of a quality, characteristic, or ability you have tended to envy in others that has caused you to struggle with the ability to be content with your own reality? List as many as you can think of. For each one, list beside it one of your own personal strengths. Give yourself permission to be your own person, be thankful for the strengths of others, and look for ways your strengths can complement the weaknesses of others, or how your weakness can be helped by others' strength.

Example:

- Have wished I could be a persuasive speaker   I am a loyal friend.

- Have wanted to be known for being funny   People trust me.
- Wished I was skilled in creating new ideas   I manage multiple tasks well.
- Wish I could lead corporations   I am good with small teams.

1.

2.

3.

4.

5.

If you lead a group or team, can you identify an ability or strength lacking in that team that would be an asset if present?

Example:

- We don't have someone who can ask the hard or right questions.
- We have a number of talented people, but no one who can really make us feel like a team.
- We have a strong male perspective but no female input.
- We lack a vision caster or someone who can see the big picture.

1.

2.

3.

4.

5.

ACTION STEPS

1. Consider whether there are ways to address personal weaknesses you have identified.

   Example:

• Not very good at public speaking	Take a course on speaking
• Always late for appointments	Practice leaving ten minutes early
• Don't work well under pressure	Take course or read resources on time management
• Impatient	Practice being a good listener before responding

2. Consider whether there are ways to address areas of weakness on your team or within the group of people you lead.

   Example:

   - Add one or more women to the team.
   - Add someone who can organize team activities.
   - Take training as a team on functioning as a team.
   - Look for someone who is strong at listening and discerning.
   - Add someone who is a strong administrator.

five

KNOW YOUR PERSONALITY

"Until you make peace with who you are . . .
you'll never be content with what you have."
—Doris Mortman, author

Leadership Lesson

You have a personality that makes you uniquely different from many others. Understanding the basic personality traits in yourself and others will greatly enhance your relationship to others and your ability to lead them.

Who have you dreamed about being more like, or who have you wished you could be? I have had a lifelong interest in the historical American West. I am especially drawn to the period from about 1850 to 1910, when so much of the western United States was being explored, settled, and influenced by nineteenth and early twentieth century civilization. It was a time when great changes in society and developments in technology and transportation essentially brought the era of the "old west" to a close. I really enjoyed reading magazines and watching television programs and movies with stories about the American West, although they often were historically inaccurate and glamorized for Hollywood audiences.

As I watched these heroic characters tame the West, uphold the law, subdue outlaws, and capture the hearts of women (who I'm now convinced were, in reality, significantly more beautiful and tantalizing than most pioneer women), I thought of these heroes as men who were worth imitating. In real life, as my experience and maturity grew, I became increasingly aware that their magnetism was a product of a script, and their real lives were not always as desirable as I had believed. However, as I was drawn into these stories, they not only provided me with many hours of entertainment, but also caused me to think about things I saw in others that were desirable and admirable.

No doubt you have had experiences where you have looked at others and wished you could be like them. It may have been because they were always the life of the party and you were not. Perhaps you admired their way of relating to others and making others feel special. It may have been that they had a great sense of humor and seemed to always have a quick and witty response to others' comments. They may have been people who showed great compassion for others and identified with the needs of those around them. Perhaps they showed an unusual ability to remain calm and composed in the face of circumstances that would make most others, yourself included, come apart at the seams. There could be a number of people whom, for a variety of reasons, you have admired, respected, and wished you could be like.

To see qualities in others you admire and to desire to show more of those qualities in your own life is natural and worthy. This becomes problematic, though, when wanting to be someone else is no longer the innocent dreaming of a young child but an ongoing struggle carried into adulthood. When you fixate more on what you wish you were than on appreciating what you are, you weaken your ability to enjoy the life you have, and you certainly limit your ability to lead well. Yet it seems that many leaders have a minimal understanding, at best, of whom they really are at the core or a minimal appreciation of what makes them unique. You may be one of them, as I was for many years.

When you fail to have a strong understanding or a clear picture of your personality, you will fail to capitalize on that knowledge as a strength. The result can be the experience of an ongoing string of below-average achievements, a series of failed efforts, short-term relationships, or short-lived vocational experiences. The culprit isn't your lack of talent or inability to be successful, it's your ongoing effort to live and lead in ways that do not represent who you are at the core.

I've had vivid reminders of this in my own life, which have been unenjoyable experiences but good teachers. One of those was my attempt during my college years to be a door-to-door cutlery salesman. I received special training, bought the sampler kit, was motivated by the success of others, and was enthused about achieving great sales that would earn my way through college. It did not take but a few door-to-door calls to realize that I absolutely hated the business and could not sell a knife if my life depended on it. (Actually, I did sell a paring knife, but the commission on that knife had no negligible effect on my tuition expenses.) I was ready to quit, but my father saw the opportunity for a life lesson (fathers do that sometimes, though we'd rather they didn't) and told me I had to make at least ten house calls a day before coming home. My distaste for the business of door-to-door selling was so great that I deliberately looked for homes where it appeared no one was there, would knock, leave, repeat that ten times, and would then be homeward bound! The experience probably helped build determination in me to push through difficult circumstances, but it also taught me that I was not going to be able to make a living selling anything door-to-door.

Why did I find it such a difficult task to do what others seemed to accomplish so naturally? A big part of the answer is that I do not have a personality that is given to that kind of activity. I'm just not a salesperson. I didn't fully understand it then (though I had a pretty good idea), but I understand more clearly now that people with certain types of personalities make great salespeople.

Think about it. What have been the experiences you have had that you found distasteful or difficult, and at which you could not seem to succeed or even enjoy as much as others? There could be a variety of reasons, such as lack of training, unpleasant supervisors, or a lack of support in that role. It could also have been because that experience clashed with your personality!

As a unique person, you have a personality that is not like everyone else's. To live and lead successfully, you must learn to live with an appreciation and acceptance of who you are. And although you are imperfect like the rest of us and need to continue growing, you represent a unique and special package as a person. You may find that difficult to believe or accept if you are struggling with background issues of self-esteem due to the words or actions of others, or if you received more criticism in your past than affirmation. However, learn to accept that you have a personality and qualities that are not like everyone else's and which can be a blessing to yourself and others.

One of the ways to discover insights into who you are is through the experiences of life and the lessons learned through those experiences.

However, those insights will be limited. You may suspect certain things about yourself, but you may have difficulty getting a complete picture without exploring a few outside sources of wisdom, such as personality assessment tools. Over the years I have taken several. The value of doing multiple assessments is that they have confirmed certain things about my personality, and in some cases have given insights that were not as obvious in other assessments.

In some cases, trained people administer and interpret specific assessment tools for you. Such sources can be particularly insightful in understanding yourself because others can see you more objectively than you can. Through their training, they are able to bring much insight into the results. We arranged a personality assessment for each of our children, which gave them insights into their uniqueness but also ideas of vocational fields that might suit them best. On another occasion, a skilled personality assessor administered a tool to each person on our office staff and not only interpreted our personal characteristics, but also showed how those characteristics tended to interplay with the characteristics of the others on staff.

An exercise like this in any organization would be incredibly useful in building teamwork and increasing the effectiveness of that team. When you can better understand not only yourself but those around you, your capacity for relating to one other and working together is vastly improved. On the other hand, when you lack such understanding, it is easy to become frustrated and dissatisfied and to see motivation eroded. This is the very reason so many people leave marriages, jobs, and potential opportunities hoping to find a better situation. In fact, they simply carry their own inadequacies, weaknesses, and lack of understanding into a new situation, which often turns out to be just as dissatisfying as the last.

There are a number of options for personality assessments available, some of which can be self-administered, while others will need to be administered and interpreted by trained personnel. I will not include an exhaustive list or go into great detail about them, but for the benefit of those who need at least some basic information in order to have a starting point, I will briefly mention three which can be helpful.

1.   One of the most helpful resources I have found is called the Myers-Briggs Indicator. It can be taken online for a very reasonable price through various websites, and the price may include a consultation session. Follow up is available for individuals and for teams. The tool helps you understand your own personality against a grid of sixteen different personality types, such as whether you are:

Extroverted or Introverted? Do you get your energy from other people, or from your own internal world?

Sensing or Intuitive? Do you focus on the present and what you can see, or the future and what you can imagine?

Thinking or Feeling? Do you make decisions based on logic, or on values and people?

Judging or Perceiving? Do you prefer things structured and organized, or flexible and spontaneous?

2.   Another tool, which we have used in our organization, is called the DISC Profile, which is available online. The DISC (Dominance, Influence, Steadiness, Conscientiousness) will help you understand yourself better by identifying such things as how you respond to conflict, what motivates you, what tends to cause you stress, how you problem solve, how you can work with (or better relate to) others, and more.

3.   The Enneagram is another tool available online which matches you against nine different personality types. Although you may find some

of each in yourself, you will tend to lean toward one, and this tool will help you identify it, along with traits of each of those nine personality types.

A simple search of the web will lead to these and a host of other potential personality assessment tools, some for free and others for a nominal cost, with most taking minimal time. Each of these will have its strengths and limitations, but any of them will be helpful and useful in better understanding the unique person you are. Taking the time to participate in one or more of these will be a great step forward in truly understanding yourself.

For Individual Consideration or Group Discussion

Identify at least two people you admire, write their names below, list reasons you admire them, and consider whether those reasons might reflect a personality trait they have.

Example:

- Person #1: faithfulness, humor, confidence   Yes, some natural, some developed

- Person #2: good salesperson, good athlete   First one Yes, second one No

Identify at least two people below you would rather avoid, write their names below, list reasons you would prefer to avoid them, and consider whether those reasons might reflect a personality trait they have.

Example:

- Person #1: angry, impatient, insensitive   No, personal issues
- Person #2: talkative, too focused on people   Yes, highly people oriented while I can be focused on the task or goal

List below any personality traits you believe you have observed about yourself.

Example:

- I see myself as quiet, introverted, private.
- I can be a good listener.
- I like being in charge of tasks.

1.

2.

3.

4.

5.

If you have taken one or more personality assessments previously, what are some of the personal traits you recall being identified regarding yourself, and have you seen those confirmed in your daily activities and interactions?

Example:

- Extroverted: Yes, I am very people oriented and find energy in being with them.
- Detail oriented:Yes, I notice the small things like misspelled words.
- Steadiness: Yes, I can be a stabilizing influence in the midst of changes.

1.

2.

3.

4.

5.

ACTION STEPS

1. Schedule time in the next several days to do Internet research on different personality assessments available and select one that could potentially be helpful to you.

2. Talk to a human resource person in your organization for recommendations on a good personality assessment.

3. Schedule a personality assessor to work with your team in order to strengthen your understanding of yourself and one another and to enhance your team's effectiveness.

six

KNOW YOUR TEMPERAMENT

*"There are three things extremely hard: steel,
a diamond, and to know one's self."*
—*Benjamin Franklin, politician and theorist*

Leadership Lesson

You have a temperament, which tends to be your default in how you respond to life and the people and situations around you. Understanding it will make you a stronger and more effective leader, as well as aide you in your relationships.

If you look for information on the web concerning human temperament, you will find the words often associated with personality. A quick search for temperament analysis tools will lead to some of the very same tools mentioned in the previous chapter, such as the DISC Profile, the Enneagram, and the Myers-Briggs Indicator. While there is overlap in speaking of personality and temperament, one needs to approach the two with the understanding that personality and temperament are very interrelated; yet, they are not two words for the same thing. For this reason, I have dedicated a separate chapter to the discussion of temperament.

So what's the difference between temperament and personality? In its simplest terms, temperament is one aspect of a person's overall personality. Your own temperament, and those of the people you lead, has to do with how a personality is manifested through a person's attitudes, feelings, emotions, and actions. It has to do with how you behave or react to the people and circumstances around you. Behavior motivated by values is one aspect of your temperament, but so is behavior motivated by your emotional makeup or your character. It speaks of your tendencies, or what I would describe as your "default." When faced with danger or difficulty, or when dealing with difficult people, how do you tend to respond? This is an indicator of your temperament. It reveals your default reaction.

As you think about this in terms of not only your own default but also of those you lead, it has enormous ramifications for understanding and leading others. For example, could it be that the tension you are experiencing in relation to a co-worker or a team member stems from a difference of temperament? Perhaps their default when faced with stress is to panic, worry, or look for quick fixes, while your default is to step back, evaluate, and look for optional ways through the challenge. Perhaps when someone in your organization is failing to pull their weight, the reaction of certain individuals on your team is anger, which leads to deteriorating relationships. However, your own response may be to tactfully and honestly confront the situation with the good of that person, as well as the team, in mind.

Differing temperaments on a team can be a strength, or a source of conflict. I have served on a number of teams, both under another's leadership and as the one leading, and have seen temperaments produce both positive results and also conflict.

When I was newly married, one of my first jobs was as an assistant to a legislator for the state of Oregon, largely doing research on key subjects of importance to him. I can recall being hired without meeting my new boss, and I was excited about the future (especially since I had graduated with a bachelor's degree in political science). I was ready to take on the challenge.

Very soon after being hired, I remember the legislator's office contacting me to set up a lunch meeting where I would meet with my new boss, who lived in another part of the state. I looked forward to it with anticipation, and on the day of the meeting, I made my way to the cafeteria at the capitol building where we were to meet. We quickly selected our lunch items and made our way to a table. In my mind, this was an opportunity to get to know each other a bit so we could enhance our working relationship. It would also be an opportune time to talk in more detail about the expectations of my job. Within moments of the beginning of our conversation, it was obvious that he wasn't interested in anything personal whatsoever, and the opportunity to talk about the future and expectations of my job quickly became a verbal lashing by my employer for outcomes he felt were less than satisfactory, but which had not been clarified to me. My new employer's strictly corporate and aggressive manner was a stark contrast to what I had expected and hoped for. It left me so emotionally devastated that I can remember returning home and sitting on the floor for the next three or four hours, simply trying to recover from the experience and figure out what had just happened.

A difference of personality? Yes! A difference in leadership styles? Yes! A difference in understanding and expectations? You bet!

However, the encounter (which was a large contributor to the short duration of that particular job) also represented a difference in temperaments. For my employer, it was strictly business, and his default manner tended toward high expectation, low emotion, and huge assumptions that I should somehow know what to do and should just do it. For me, emotions and expectations clashed with the experience and, while he walked away somewhat angry, I walked away emotionally drained and feeling like I'd been hit by a truck.

When personalities and temperaments clash, or at least manifest themselves differently, the potential for either a productive or destructive outcome coexists, which is why it is extremely helpful to understand your own personal default temperament as well as those of others with whom you live, work, or associate with in a variety of contexts. To that end, the personality tools I mentioned earlier can be very insightful.

Another such tool is called The Keirsey Temperament Sorter (http://www.keirsey.com). This particular tool characterizes people as guardians, idealists, artisans, or rationals. As with personality differences, there can be an overlap in which you can identify with elements of more than one category, but you will lean most strongly toward one of those. Tied closely to The Myers-Briggs Indicator, The Keirsey Temperament Sorter offers four types of people under each of the four major temperaments. One of the strengths of this tool is that overviews and assessments can be composed for yourself, your team, or your organization.

Still another great tool is the Personal Style Indicator (PSI), offered by Consulting Resource Group International, Inc. (http://www.crgleader.com). This scientifically developed, self-administered, self-scoring instrument can effectively clarify your tendencies in responding to people, tasks, situations, and stress, and it helps identify your preferred work style and environment, as well as the impact of your default tendencies on others. Further, these insights help in understanding others' default tendencies so you can find a greater ability to function in relation to them. The PSI is a helpful assessment tool for individuals and teams, and it can be facilitated by a professional, if desired. Scoring is based on words you feel most identify your likeness to four style dimensions. Their related Job Style Indicator (JSI) is a helpful complimentary tool, especially for those responsible in hiring others. It helps define not only the work style requirements of a role, but it gives clarity to the compatibility between an individual and that role.

Another way of viewing temperaments is through a matrix resulting from the attempts of the ancient Greeks to understand and map differing moods. These descriptors are still common in current discussion and practice. The Greeks viewed humanity as having four "moods" or temperaments:

1. **Sanguine:** The sanguine person can tend to be extroverted and social, though alone time is also important. They are creative, and can struggle with follow-through of tasks. They can be forgetful, chronically late for appointments, as well as sarcastic. They make good friends and often become lifelong friends. They exhibit enthusiasm and are energetic starters. They love popularity, performing, and are curious types. They can seem easy going and carefree and can be natural leaders. They tend toward positive feelings.

2. **Choleric:** These are doers—energetic, passionate, ambitious, aggressive. They can be leaders and like to be in charge, which is why this temperament characterizes many military leaders and politicians. It also tends to show up in times of emergency. A choleric person is faithful, brave, and enjoys the freedom of being on their own. Their

tendency is to want to bring change, and they tend to be well organized and oriented toward goals. They are strong willed, and friendships are not a high need. They lean toward negative feelings, can be anxious, impulsive, touchy, or excitable.

3. **Melancholic:** A melancholic person is a sensitive person. They are considerate and can worry about being late. They can excel in creative ways, such as poetry or art. They are thoughtful, a ponderer, and can be occupied with the tragedies and difficulties of the world. They can be a perfectionist and love details and can embrace independence and self-reliance, to the point of forgetting to think about others. They can seem analytical, serious. They, too, can lean toward negative feelings, often manifesting moodiness, pessimism, depression, rigidity, and can appear quiet and unsociable.

4. **Phlegmatic:** A phlegmatic is generally kind, accepting, affectionate, and easy to relate to. They like stability over change and can appear shy. They can lean toward being a peaceful and relaxed person, being rational and observant, which makes them good administrators. They are patient and compassionate toward others. They tend to remain calm and exhibit humility and control. They can be good listeners, and generally seem happy with their life. They may exhibit low energy and lean toward positive feelings.

You can learn more about these moods, and various tools for assessing your own temperament, by a search of the web or at your local library. While my intent is not to be exhaustive or authoritative on these descriptors, they serve to remind that everyone is not like you. That may seem an obvious overstatement, but its importance must not be underestimated.

Ways of responding to the daily encounters of life are different for you, your family, those you lead, and those you encounter in every facet of life. That doesn't make your response, or theirs, necessarily right or wrong (although there are certainly wrongful ways of expressing one's self), but simply different. If you can take a basic understanding of the differences into account, potential conflicts can be minimized, relational difficulties can be overcome, teams can be made stronger, and outcomes for you (and those you impact) can significantly weigh in favor of being opportunities for growth, understanding, and greater effectiveness.

For Individual Consideration or Group Discussion

In large part, do any of the "mood" descriptions potentially describe you? List those that apply.

- Sanguine: e.g., social, creative, forgetful
- Choleric: e.g., passionate, ambitious, well-organized
- Melancholic: e.g., artistic, perfectionist, self-reliant
- Phlegmatic: e.g., affectionate, relaxed, administrative

If you have taken a temperament analysis, such as the DISC Profile or Myers-Briggs, list as many words that described you as you can recall.

1.

2.

3.

4.

5.

Identify two people, one whom you get along with well and another whom you may have a difficult relationship with, and list the four Greek "mood" (temperament) descriptors beside their names. For each of the two people, beside the mood descriptors, write any of the temperament characteristics listed in the chapter, and consider how their temperament and yours are helped or hindered by the differences in temperament between the two of you.

Example:

- Person #1   Sanguine: extroverted, social, helps me step out of my introverted side, good friend, easy going, helps me balance my high stress
                Choleric:
                Melancholic:
                Phlegmatic: kind, peaceful, considerate, the kind of friend I need

ACTION STEPS

1. Take the online Personal Style Indicator at http://www.crgleader.com or bring in their personnel to assess and interpret your team, or do the same with the Keirsey Temperament Sorter at http://www.keirsey.com.

2. Read further on the sanguine, choleric, melancholic, and phlegmatic temperament descriptors. A simple Internet search using any of these four descriptor words will bring you to a variety of sources for further information. A free temperament analysis using these descriptors is available at http://personality-testing.info/tests/4T.php.

seven

KNOW YOUR PASSIONS

"Be a first-rate version of yourself,
not a second-rate version of someone else."
—Judy Garland, singer and actress

Leadership Lesson

Within you are one or more passions that need to be discovered, directed, and developed because they will bring energy and effectiveness to your life and work.

The words above, though spoken by a person now deceased, live on as a tremendous bit of advice to each of us. It is perhaps the struggle of every person alive to occasionally wish they were someone else, or worse yet, to try to live as if they were someone else, finding the effort frustrating and of little effect because who they are differs from who they are trying to be.

For the most part, I was happy with my youth and have appreciated my adult years. However, my acceptance of who I am as a person and a leader and learning to capitalize on that, instead of agonizing that I did not seem to get the results of others whom I admired, came only later in life. For many, that point of acceptance comes earlier, but for you, or others, it may never come without an honest, accepting look at who you are and who you are not.

In speaking of our personal passions, we come to what I call the third element in a trilogy comprised of personality, temperament, and passions. (The discussion of this chapter also cannot be separated from the subject of your life setting in Chapter 8.) You have inner passions that reflect desires, concerns, and motivations that need to be expressed in the unique context of your own life. I am speaking about more than a general concern or general appeal, which may stimulate your interest but not your actual activity. A personal passion is something that will, in some way, need to be expressed through action or activity. What is it that especially compels YOU? What is it that stirs your own emotions and desires? And have you surrounded yourself with others who, to some degree, reflect those passions, or do they tend to be people who are simply fulfilling job descriptions or the lowest level of expectations? Are you in a role that reflects those passions, or if not, are you finding ways outside your vocational, organizational context to express those inner motivations?

Passions can be innately part of you since the time you were born, or they can be born from experience. The former can be represented by the person who has since a very young age been clear and unwavering about what their vocation in life was to be. I do not represent that fortunate category of people, though I have known a few like this. They are compelled by an inner conviction that seems as much a part of their personality and temperament as whether they are an extrovert or introvert, a sanguine or a choleric. It is simply part of their fiber, and they seem born to that destiny.

On the other hand, numerous passions, while being influenced by the personality and temperament you are born with, can also be products of your life experiences. In any case, a passion yearns for expression in tangible ways. For instance, many people who become exposed first hand to the suffering of the homeless or children orphaned by war or the AIDS epidemic or the trafficking of human beings or the destruction of addictive drugs come away from the experience jolted by their compassion for others, convinced they "have to do something" to alleviate such suffering.

The options for response are as diverse as the causes of their passionate need to respond. I have friends who have chosen to respond by adopting orphans from overseas or taking in foster children from their own community. Others have been so moved that they have left their current occupations to join organizations that specifically reach out to suffering people worldwide. Still others have initiated, or joined, efforts to feed the hungry in their own region, gather clothing for needy families, or assist those devastated from the breakup of marriages or other significant losses, such as the death of someone close. These are only a few examples of passions put into action, of inner motivations that reflect the values, compassion, or convictions that compel a person to make a difference or to do something, anything, in order to express that passion.

A personal passion may be something that is sensed but cannot yet be clearly articulated. You may have an inclination toward something, or have been exposed to an activity that has made you think it might be something you would enjoy or find especially fulfilling. You may have volunteered for an activity out of a sense of responsibility, but found it stirred you inside in ways you had not expected. To have a willing spirit in being open to new experiences can lead an individual into involvements, even job choices, that express an inner passion which they previously had either been unaware of or unable to articulate. To discover a personal passion may cause a leader to find ways through their vocation or organization to incorporate that passion, making their leadership more fulfilling and impactful.

A passion may be something best expressed through a hobby, something you don't have to dedicate your entire life and every moment of the day to. My close friend Tom has realized more than one driving passion in his life, and has found a means to express those passions in ways which complement and even overlap. As a former college football player for Ohio State, and a professional football player for several years, his passion for sports compels him, and influenced his decision to develop an organization that manages community sports arenas and complexes. He has also coached community teams.

However, to some degree, Tom's chosen profession is also a reflection of an inner passion for kids and families, a motivation cultivated in him through years of being bounced from one foster home to the next, abused in some cases, hurting deeply within, until being adopted by a wonderful and loving family. His passion for kids and parenting kids has motivated him to not only become a good father to his own children, but it has influenced his vocation, as well as his extracurricular activities. He has published a book called *Man Shoes*, describing his life journey and encouraging men in their roles as fathers. He has also created a family devoted website. Through these, Tom is developing opportunities to speak to others about themes that reflect these inner motivations.

Could it be that your passion is strongly contributing to your being an effective leader? Conversely, could it be that the frustration you are experiencing in your leadership is due to the absence of a means by which to express your personal passion? For instance, a successful insurance agency may be led by people who are motivated by a desire to help others in the hard moments of life. A successful political leader may be motivated by a desire to address minority concerns. Effective spiritual leaders are primarily so because of a passion for the souls of others and for the expressions of others' spirituality.

Leadership that is motivated by personal passion is an unequalled force. Admittedly, unless the equation also includes other factors, such as integrity of character, wisdom, personal ability, and a few other positive components, passion can drive a person to unsuccessful and even disastrous effects. The critical thought for our purposes, however, is to never underestimate the importance of passion to being effective and fulfilled in your life and your leadership.

Passion in leading others not only motivates you as a leader, but it is contagious to those you lead. A person who is passionate about their activities and is expressing that passion in a positive manner is an exciting and enjoyable person to be around! Your passion stimulates others, fueling their passion, as well. Or perhaps it leads them to find ways to be supportive of you because of how your passion encourages them.

The expression of passion in constructive ways will make you a more motivated and motivating leader. Many of us can remember the impact of leaders, such as Dr. Martin Luther King, Jr., who influenced a revolution in the United States. His conviction about civil rights, expressed passionately in his "I Have a Dream" speech stirs my emotions to this day. The power of a passion expressed in a leader's life is transforming to that leader and is motivating to others! The dynamic of a personal passion matched with a personal expression of leadership is a motivator critically needed in professional, as well as volunteer, organizations. It will impact others in ways that will powerfully influence them as you partner together to achieve desirable and beneficial outcomes.

For Individual Consideration or Group Discussion

What activity or involvement do you find yourself thinking often about or has you dreaming about possibilities?

Example:

- Helping the poor
- Providing for orphans
- Owning a business
- Assisting senior citizens
- Getting involved in local or regional government

Make a list of activities or skills you are good at. Then identify one or two you are most drawn to.

1.

2.

3.

4.

5.

What involvements, activities, or possibilities do you find yourself talking about frequently because they are of interest to you?

1.

2.

3.

4.

5.

How does a personal passion influence your work, or how you spend your nonwork hours?

Example:

- My passion for people → My work allows lots of interaction and time with people.
- My passion for the poor → I volunteer at a shelter for the homeless.

ACTION STEPS

1. Research which organizations locally or outside your community might have a focus on a special area of interest for you, and consider ways you could be involved.

2. If you are unsure about a potential area of passion, but would like to explore it further, volunteer some time to an organization that could give you practical exposure to specific community activities.

3. Sign up for lessons or classes to further develop a special area of interest.

4. Apply for jobs that would allow you to exercise your area of passion.

eight

KNOW YOUR SETTING

*"It is the chiefest point of happiness that a man is
willing to be what he is."*
—Desiderius Erasmus, theologian and reformer

Leadership Lesson

**Your setting, and how you fit or function within it, will play a
vital role in your effectiveness as a leader.**

One of the greatest athletes of recent years is professional basketball
superstar Steve Nash. Steve is an incredible talent on the basketball court,
and he has generated a lot of excitement for the sport, as well as helped
sell a lot of tickets whenever his team competes. Born in South Africa, but
raised in Canada, he developed significantly in his teen years as a player
for his Canadian high school, but he was further honed when he attended

an American university on a basketball scholarship. He was a key player for the team and was twice named player of the year for the West Coast Conference.

Upon graduation, Steve entered the NBA draft and was picked up by the Phoenix Suns. His dream of being a professional basketball player had become a reality. However, his initial excursion into the NBA was fairly unimpressive, and two years later, he was traded to the Dallas Mavericks. He improved and became a real contributor to that team, helping lead them to the conference finals. He became a free agent in the '03–'04 season, though, and his pathway again merged with the Phoenix Suns, where he played the next several years. In 2006, ESPN named Steve the ninth best point guard in NBA history, and that same year, due to his leadership on the basketball court as well as his philanthropic works, *Time Magazine* honored him among the most influential one hundred people on earth. The following year, he was awarded one of the highest honors in Canada, the Order of Canada.

As an NBA All-Star, Nash has made a great impact both on and off the basketball court. I remember reading a commentator's article in 2011 in which he speculated that it may be time for Nash to find another team. Although his personal statistics were good, and his talent was perhaps better than ever, he found himself in a context where his own talent was not complimented by that of others, and the Suns found themselves continuing in a downward spiral.

For a player like Nash, that can lead to nagging questions, such as: Is this team the best fit for me? Is this where I can make my best impact? Does this team have the potential to be the competitors I long to be associated with? What will it take to change the situation? Can I continue to grow and develop here? His experience brought him to a crossroads of decision. He had never won an NBA Championship, and in what was believed to be a decision motivated by that goal, the start of the 2012–13 NBA season found Nash playing for the Los Angeles Lakers alongside other great stars of the game.

Steve Nash's story is unique to himself. However, his experience is not. You have faced, and may be currently facing, situations in which you have had to take a hard look at the situation in which you found yourself and have had to ask probing questions. Multiple times in my own leadership experience I have come to such a crossroads, and I have had to determine whether continuing on in my job role was the path I should take. Each of these circumstances involved factors that drove me to evaluate whether it was going to continue being a place in which my leadership would be needed, fruitful, or desirable. This is not to advocate an attitude of "bailing out" when difficulty arises, but situations change, as do people, and there are times when, for good reasons, it is preferable to change your setting.

In my own experience, there have always been several factors, not just one, which converge to create a picture suggesting that another situation would be better for the next phase of my life and leadership. Factors have included family needs, financial restraints, professional development opportunities, a desire to lead in ways not abundantly present in the current situation, changing makeup and responsibilities within the team, changes within the organization itself, and other factors or limitations. In more than one of those situations, I came to a conclusion that while I could continue on, it would only lead to greater frustration and possible stagnation.

Can you recall a time like that in your own experience? Are you facing current realities that are making you question whether it is the place you should, or want, to remain? Such important decisions should not be made lightly, impulsively, or without a great deal of consideration and discussion with your spouse, as well as other trusted sources.

What supports or hinders your leadership where you are currently? Does your setting seem to be a good fit for your strengths, personality, temperament, and passions? Perhaps in the beginning it was, but things have changed. Or perhaps YOU have changed, and as you have continued growing as an individual and a leader, your current situation has not kept pace with your growing leadership ability and interests. William Shakespeare penned these words: "This above all: to thine own self be true." Does your current setting support and draw out the real you?

It could be that you still fit the need or the role, but you don't have the kind of people around you who can help you take your team or organization where it needs to go. If so, hard questions have to again be asked about whether some of those on your team can continue to contribute there, or whether new additions to the team are necessary. I have seen great environment created and great results achieved in teams that seemed to fit the need and fit well with each other. On the other hand, I have observed teams deteriorate and results limited, even dissipated, when one or more members of the team do not seem to fit their role, clash with other members of the team, or they resist change (even though change is inevitable in personal, as well as organizational, life).

Perhaps as mentioned your organization, or situation, has changed significantly but you no longer seem to fit. Yet because of your dislike for change, you determine to carry on, preferring the security of the familiar to the potential opportunities (and risk) involved in seeking another role or environment. A decision to stay in a situation you no longer fit can not only frustrate you but also those around you, because your lack of motivation and enthusiasm for the activities of that team can be infectious to others. Admittedly, there are periods of time when each of us has to carry on in a situation that is less than ideal. Sometimes, there are no readily available or viable alternatives. It will be important to address the situation from the standpoint of the big picture, the long-term one. Even if it is necessary to continue in that situation for a time, what would be the impact on you and those around you if you continued indefinitely or long term?

As you evaluate your circumstance, and whether you believe it best supports who you are and what you have to offer, realize that there are potentially a number of situations or settings in which your abilities and potential could be developed. Realize, too, there are a number of factors you should consider when looking at whether a given situation may be your best option. Consider:

- Does your organization have others who work over you and under you who share passionately in the organization's vision?
- Is there potential for ongoing professional development and growth as a leader?
- Is the area where you live is a good match for your own interests and passions?
- What is the makeup of your team, and are you are at your best in leading a team, or working as a subordinate to another?
- Can you see yourself thriving and excelling in your present circumstance if you stayed there another ten years?
- Does your current circumstance challenge you and prompt you to keep learning?
- Is there another role that would fit you better, and is there opportunity to step into such a role?
- Do you find your role (or the environment in which you exercise it) energizing, or demoralizing and draining?
- Are you in need of a mentor?
- Do you feel isolated and unable to meet expectations?

Many questions could serve as illustrations of the kind of factors that may indicate the kind of situation or role that best fits you and whether you are in such a circumstance.

If asking these questions affirms that you are in a setting that fits who you are, then move ahead with confidence and renewed commitment. However, if asking questions like these affirms that you are not in such a setting, begin evaluating what kind of changes might be needed in you, your role, or your organization in order to produce a better fit, or whether that is even possible in your current situation. It may be that in the short term you will need to continue without change for financial or other reasons. Yet it can also be an opportunity to establish goals for the future and begin taking steps that will produce a harvest of reward and greater effectiveness in the years to come!

For Individual Consideration or Group Discussion

What are words you would use to describe your current vocational role?

Example:

- Exciting, fulfilling, boring, frustrating, unrewarding, challenging, terrible, fitting

List reasons for the words you have chosen to describe your current vocational context.

Example:

- Exciting: I meet lots of interesting people.
- Fulfilling: I feel like I'm making a difference.
- Boring: There's no challenge to it; it's always the same.
- Frustrating: My supervisor and I don't agree on anything.
- Unrewarding: It doesn't make life better for me or others.
- Challenging: I don't feel equipped to meet the expectations.
- Terrible: It doesn't appeal to me at all.
- Fitting: I feel like it fits my interests and abilities.

If there are aspects to your setting that you struggle with, do you think it is because your situation has changed, or you have changed, or perhaps both?

Example:

- It doesn't seem challenging anymore. → I have grown in my abilities.
- It doesn't feel warm and personal now. → The number of people has increased.
- I feel like it's constantly changing. → I need more training to improve my skills.
- Our team doesn't feel close. → Several new members have joined.

What would be the greatest challenges to making needed changes in your situation?

Example:

- Finding time to enhance my skills with my busy schedule
- Not having enough money saved for an extended job search if unemployed
- Convincing others that we need to do some real relationship building
- Having to fire a person I really like
- Learning to say "no" to what drains me or "yes" to what brings me energy

1.

2.

3.

4.

5.

ACTION STEPS

1. Explore seminars, classes, books, or other means of developing your abilities.

2. Volunteer to take on additional responsibilities.

3. Receive career counseling.

4. Invite others to spend time with you in enjoyable activities in order to get to know them better and strengthen those relationships.

5. Ask yourself: What is my context teaching me about myself that is affirming or helpful?

nine

KNOW YOUR SPIRITUAL SELF

"The failure of leaders to deal with their own souls, their inner life, is deeply troubling not only for themselves but also for other persons in the misery they cause. The destructive consequences from leaders who fail to work out of a deep sense of their inner self are staggering. . . . Leaders have a particular responsibility to know what is going on inside their souls. For leaders, this means taking the journey in and down. As they become fully awake, they come to know and understand what it is within that betrays them and those they strive to serve."
—*Patricia D. Brown, author of Learning to Lead from Your Spiritual Center*

Leadership Lesson

Knowing yourself spiritually will vastly impact your personal experience and your leadership effectiveness.

No matter where you go in the world, you will find people engaged in expressions of spirituality that are diverse, personal, and deeply meaningful. In some settings, it may be manifested through certain activities intended to pacify evil spirits or honor departed ancestors. It appears elsewhere as gatherings of groups of people in churches, temples, homes, or other venues where they engage in various forms of worship, teaching, prayers, as well as other means of seeking community with God and others. For some, their dissatisfaction with the material world convinces them there must be something more satisfying and fulfilling than the tangible world and leads them to engage in the pursuit of something transcendental, something that goes beyond their normal experience, something that touches them at the level of their soul.

Discussions between people commonly center on matters related to death and the contemplation of whether there is some form of existence beyond death and what that might entail. The very fear of death drives people the world over to engage in practices aimed at avoiding, or at least delaying, death. One of the more recently developed offerings of those catering to tourists in select locations, and the subject of many a television program, is "ghost tours," or experiences in haunted venues where the spirits of departed and restless souls supposedly linger.

These are but a few examples of the many, many ways we express, in natural and supernatural ways, our awareness of a spiritual, unseen dimension to life. Some sincerely believe that humanity's existence is merely a physical experience that relates to nothing greater, nothing more lasting than a few short years on earth, and then nothingness. Others believe that life on this earth is a fading fluke that is nothing more than the temporary gathering of a few cells into human, animal, and plant forms. However, most of us have a deep sense there is something more to the picture.

I would place myself in the latter category. In my own experience, as well as the experience of thousands I have known or observed, not to mention through the writings of others through the ages, I have become more and more aware that just as there is a physical aspect to human beings that relates to their exterior body and its inner components, and just as there is also a mental aspect which relates to the inner thoughts and the processes of the mind, so too is there a spiritual aspect to us all.

This spiritual aspect of your humanity relates to your soul and to your magnetic pull toward something beyond yourself. For me, it has involved a journey that largely started in my teen years, but has been an ongoing growth in understanding myself, God, and my relationship to Him. My journey has continued even as a spiritual leader, through my involvement in various Christian churches, both as a member and as a pastor, as well as my association and cooperative work with people in many Christian organizations and denominations. It has led me into roles that have involved working with a diversity of people across North America and from around the world. It has been fed by personal studies, as well as formal studies, which resulted ultimately in a doctoral degree focused on leadership and spiritual formation.

The expression of your own spirituality may be quite different from mine, and my point in this chapter is not to argue one expression over another. It is, though, to remind you that the spiritual element to your life and the reality of a soul within you makes it of paramount importance that you recognize that in addition to the physical and mental aspects of your existence, you are a spiritual being.

My own belief system, based on the Bible, holds to the view that God created us for fellowship with Him. Further, I believe that the inner longings for a purposeful life and for the meaning of one's life, as well as the diverse expressions of spirituality I mentioned earlier, are reflections of our inner spiritual longing for God. We may choose to deny God, or deny that these longings are ultimately a desire to know God, but we cannot deny these longings exist, and to ignore this reality is to stifle the deepest aspect of who you are as a human being.

To ignore the idea that you and those you lead are spiritual beings is to stunt your potential as a person and as a leader. It would also mean missing what can motivate you or others in making many choices and decisions, as well as what sometimes may lead to actions that can be counterproductive to personal development and leadership.

The reality and importance of the spiritual aspect of life is a theme unrestricted to religious leaders or people of faith, or, for that matter, to any particular vocation or persuasion. You can look to numerous writers, such as the nineteenth century English writer, James Allen, who spoke of the inner spiritual self when he stated, "Only by much searching and mining are gold and diamonds obtained, and man can find every truth connected with his being if he will dig deep into the mine of his soul."[1]

Blaise Pascal, a man with a brilliant mind, was a seventeenth-century French writer, physicist, inventor, and mathematician, among other things, and he strongly influenced developments in the social sciences, as well as modern economics. Pascal defended what has been referred to as the scientific method. He later turned his interests to philosophy and theology. In his earlier scientific work, he had a special interest in the existence of vacuums within the natural world, which you could speculate influenced his description of a vacuum in human hearts that only God could fill. Pascal's reference to God was his understanding of God as made known to us by Jesus Christ.

1.　James Allen, available from http://www.self-improvement-success.com/self-aware-ness-quotes.html.

There are many who would say that there is a yearning for God deep within us all, and no matter what we do to try to suppress it, that yearning is an inseparable part of our being.

Why is this so important to you, and to understanding yourself? In finding God, you find yourself! This is not to suggest that man is God, which I do not believe, but it is to suggest that your own identity and purpose cannot be ultimately separated from the consideration of God. Another way of stating it would be: in coming to know God, you come to better know yourself, and by better knowing yourself, you can better know others. The importance of this knowledge extends vastly beyond the purposes of this chapter, so I will comment on two things of value to this discussion. The first is the value to you as an individual in being able to address the struggles and concerns of your daily life, and for those who believe, to be able to find hope that transcends the circumstances of your life as you are pointed to an even more meaningful life beyond this one. The second value, equally important and perhaps more focused to our purposes here, is the value to you as a leader.

For a number of reasons, your inner spiritual life is important to your effectual leadership. Your spiritual life reminds you there is more to this life than what you can see, earn, or control. This helps you keep perspective and encourages a humility in your leadership by remembering there's a bigger picture, that life isn't just about you or the little bits of reality that physically surround you. It also prompts you to keep learning, realizing there is so much more you do not know. This is critical because leaders need to be ongoing learners!

Further, if you're a Christian leader, your faith calls you to be the kind of leader Christ was: a servant leader, using his leadership for the good of others and the meeting of needs. Your faith also provides your greatest resource for the challenges of leadership, which are numerous, diverse, and sometimes painful. In finding hope for the soul, you can also find a greater purpose and passion in your leading.

Many organizations are recognizing the importance of spirituality in the workplace and are supporting people's recognition of themselves as spiritual beings. This is the reason for the increasing number of business organizations hiring multi-faith chaplains. The armed forces have long used chaplains of various faiths, as do many penitentiaries and other penal-type institutions.

As a final note, I want to speak to leaders on an organizational level. I find the following words from the International Institute for Spiritual Leadership of considerable interest. Whether one is a Christian, a person of another faith, or of no faith, these words are significant:

> "A major change is also taking place in the personal and professional lives of leaders as many of them more deeply integrate their spirituality and their work. Most would agree that this integration is leading to very positive changes in their relationships and their effectiveness. There is also evidence that workplace spirituality not only leads to beneficial personal outcomes, such as increased joy, peace, serenity, job satisfaction, and commitment, but that they also deliver improved productivity and reduce absenteeism and turnover. Employees who work for organizations they consider to be spiritual are less fearful, more ethical, and more committed. And, there is mounting evidence that a more humane workplace is more productive, flexible, and creative."[2]

These words acknowledge a direct relationship between your inner spiritual life and outward effectiveness and productivity. For personal, organizational, vocational, and relational reasons, know yourself spiritually!

---

2. "Workplace Spirituality," available at http://iispiritualleadership.com/workplace-spirituality/.

For Individual Consideration or Group Discussion

Considering the quote above from the International Institute for Spiritual Leadership, what do you find of interest, and why?

Example:

- Relationship of spirituality and absenteeism → job productivity can increase.

What words would you use to describe your own spiritual journey currently?

Example:

- Interested, indifferent, hungering, curious, satisfying

List ways that your current role is, or could be, strengthened by recognition of your own spirituality and that of others?

Example:

- My organization could encourage a more creative and satisfying environment by being supportive of religious activities that benefit our community and our employees.
- Our family relationships could be more fulfilling if we shared in faith activities together.
- Our organization could benefit from the presence of a chaplain.

1.

2.

3.

4.

5.

ACTION STEPS

1. Have a meaningful conversation with someone you trust who you believe could answer some of your questions about God, faith, and spirituality.

2. Do further reading on the topic of a personal soul. Online sources, such as Wikipedia or http://www.amazon.com (word search "human soul" or "Christian theology of the soul"), and most especially the Bible, are good starting points.

3. Read biographies about people of faith.

4. If you are a person of faith, begin to daily view your life, work, and faith as integral and mutually related. List ways this perspective could affect how you live and lead.

5. Make it a more spiritually friendly environment for your team, organization, or other group you lead by allowing and inviting open dialogue about spiritual matters.

ten

KNOW YOUR LIMITS

*"The basic experience of everyone is the
experience of human limitation."*
—*Flannery O'Connor, novelist and writer*

Leadership Lesson

**You are limited by who you are and by the circumstances
in your life. Knowing your limitations and honoring them,
as well as continually working at maintaining balance, is
critical to your growth and effectiveness.**

It happened again! In the past months I've seen leaders lose their
positions of leadership, damage lives, and prematurely end their ability
to lead others toward positive outcomes because they either failed to

recognize or failed to pay heed to their limitations, instead of setting and honoring good boundaries. They went too far, and it proved their undoing. Anyone who has held positions of leadership has seen similar scenarios. I suspect that some of you reading these words have had this unfortunate experience and may still be feeling the sting of it, or are working through the effects of it.

To some degree, we all have experienced this, whether in small or large measure. We've gone too far; we've failed to set or honor boundaries; we've overextended ourselves emotionally or physically or mentally. It may have been in simpler ways, such as failure to get the rest you needed, which resulted in a weakened immune system and you fell ill. Or perhaps you failed to take times of rest and renewal, kept postponing vacations, until you wore yourself out physically and mentally and needed medical intervention or extended time off. There are numerous ways we all are prone to overstep boundaries and limitations and create situations that can harm ourselves (or others) and seriously impact our ability to lead them.

What you need is not the ability to know how close you can get to the edge of a cliff before you actually fall over. This may be exciting for a few extreme thrill seekers, but it's a dangerous game to play and you can easily lose. On the contrary, you need to gain a better understanding of your own limitations as a human being and avoiding situations that can lead you perilously close to disaster. It's true that there are times you need to take risks in leadership, and risk means stepping outside your comfort zones and outside your norm. It's also true that you sometimes don't know your limits until you've faced a situation that has tested you in ways that have forced you to realize those limits.

Furthermore, it's true that you sometimes need to push yourself toward your limits in order to achieve worthwhile dreams or goals. I also recognize that every once in awhile the human experience calls you to push beyond your limits because there is little other choice. This latter experience is what produces heroes who rush into burning houses to rescue perishing victims, or who push fear aside on the battlefield. It's also what forces some of us to go beyond our norm when disciplining our bodies during training, or to accomplish an important task by a pending deadline.

Yes, there are times when all of us will be called upon to push ourselves, and perhaps others, "to the limit" or even beyond because of special circumstances. However, if this tends to describe more of an ongoing pattern than a temporary necessity, you are pushing yourself (and perhaps others) in unhealthy directions that can have bad results, such as lost health, bad decisions and choices, burnout, or other counterproductive (if not outright destructive) effects. This is why it's so important for you to know your limitations and listen to the warning bells that go off physically, mentally, or otherwise when limits are being reached or breached.

Part of what is being said here is that there is a shadow side of leadership. Parker Palmer in *Let Your Life Speak* lists five possible shadows in leaders' lives: 1) "I am what I do"; 2) "This is a war and I must fight and win"; 3) "It all depends on me"; 4) "We won't have to deal with chaos and pain if we manage everything perfectly"; and 5) "Nothing can fail or die on my watch."[1] Each of these is worthy of at least a chapter, if not an entire book! But at the least, for our purposes, they represent some of the fallacies in leaders' thinking.

Your life and work are not warzones that boil down to personal winning, because your leadership, as much as possible, should be a win-win for others, as well as yourself. It may feel like everything depends on you, but does it really, or have you created an unhealthy situation in which

---

1   Parker Palmer, *Let Your Life Speak: Listening for the Voice of Vocation* (San Francisco: Jossey-Bass, 1999).

you have neglected to allow others to carry the load with you? No one can manage everything perfectly without failures, and chaos (as well as pain) are not only part of life and leadership, but also part of what grows and matures you. When you are driven by pride and a standard in which failure is not an option, it can set you up for a hard fall when failure becomes a reality. It also ignores the important truth that at times certain things need to die in order for other things to spring to life. When unrealistic expectations drive you, you can easily overstep limits and put yourself on an unhealthy trajectory.

Another aspect of life and leadership I am speaking to in the matter of understanding your limits is that of working constantly at keeping a reasonable balance. When I was a boy growing up in Oregon, we lived near a rail line. The tracks were perhaps no more than seventy-five yards from our house, and they became a great source of entertainment for my brothers and me. In fact, they were a little more prone than I, the first-born "responsible" one, to push the limits. Freight trains would regularly come by our house, and my younger brothers made a sport of hopping onto some of those trains and riding them for a short distance before jumping off and returning home victoriously, without my parents' awareness (until many years later).

While I thought about hopping those trains, I played it safe and instead used to enjoy walking along the tracks looking for discarded soft drink or beer bottles I could trade in for a few cents. I also enjoyed an activity that I still find myself doing occasionally, namely trying to walk on top of a rail as far as possible before falling off. I never set world records doing so, and still can only make it a limited distance before losing my balance and falling off the rail. At times I would go to great effort, with arms and legs flailing, working desperately to stay on top of the rail before losing my balance and falling. Sometimes I would try to run the rail, and my attempt at staying atop as my speed increased was usually quite short-lived.

The metaphor of balancing yourself on top of a metal rail may be a common human experience, and it's a useful picture of what happens when any of us loses our balance and ends up off-track. What kinds of things can knock you off balance and leave you feeling like you are flailing desperately? Maintaining a balance is a daily effort, and it's constantly challenging. Balance can even be a moving target, because what represents balance for one day may be different for another, or what may be required of you for a season of time may be different than other seasons. This is why it's impossible for anyone, myself included, to tell you what your own limits are or what represents balance for you in every situation.

There are numerous factors involved in determining balance and limits, such as your personality type, personal capacity or emotional frame, the state of family relationships, physical condition, circumstances at your job, personal skills, and your maturity level and experience. It's also impacted by nutritional intake, sleep patterns, and even negative influences, such as pride, addictive tendencies, levels of stress, or pressure related to work assignments. This list is not exclusive, but it probably represents some of the more critical and common factors.

Some of these you can do little about, such as personality type or job circumstances. Personal skills are predetermined in some measure, but you can also develop them to varying degrees. Some factors you can have a direct effect upon, such as nutrition, rest, physical conditioning, emotional health, and others, and you need to work at these. Some may require strong input and other people's help, and you need to be humble and honest enough to admit it and allow it. Some things, such as stress and pressure, are very much a part of life and leadership, and you cannot avoid experiencing it. What you can do, however, is to try to minimize such experiences, or at least minimize their effects, by constantly working at balance and rebalancing.

All of this is a strong reminder of the importance of self-leadership. Much has been written about this, but its importance is so great that it's worth being reminded that before you can effectively lead others, you must be able to lead yourself. When you stop leading yourself effectively, in some way or another, you are going to "fall off the rail," and the impact will not only be personal, but will also affect those around you.

I have had to be reminded of this reality in different settings throughout my career. One of the early examples was the decision to leave the first church I served as pastor for a few determining reasons, one of which was a recognition that my family was growing and that our small church was simply unable at the time to provide a salary needed to maintain my family's needs. Another reason was the need to be honest with myself and realize that as a young, inexperienced leader, I did not have what was needed to lead that church to its next stage of growth. I simply did not have the knowledge or experience necessary. For these and other reasons, my wife and I determined it was time for me to find a pastoral role elsewhere. More recently in my career, my doctoral studies were a recognition of my own state of intellectual dryness and the need for ongoing learning. The completion of those studies has enabled me to move toward the future with renewed passion and effectiveness.

For you, as well, there will be occasions when you need to know and accept your limitations. Trouble develops when you continue as-is, unwilling to accept your limitations, always trying to prove yourself to yourself or others, and continually falling short because your actions flow from who you want to be instead of accepting who you are. Further, there will be plenty of incidents that will serve to remind you that no one can be all things to all people, and you need to be comfortable with that realization.

There will also be many opportunities in which you will need to practice the important principle of knowing when to say "yes" to things that breed balance and infuse you with life and energy, or when to say "no" to things that will overload and drain you. Too, there will be times when you need to be honest with yourself and admit when further training is called for, or if it may be time to step aside and seek another opportunity. I've seen leaders who have overstayed their time, and should have known better, but ignored the indicators and reaped undesirable results.

Life is a challenge in many ways, and leadership will add to those challenges. However, knowing your limits, and honoring them, will prove immeasurably helpful in keeping you on track to growth and effectiveness in your personal life and in helping you effectively lead others.

For Individual Consideration or Group Discussion

Name at least five personal limitations.

Example:

- My ongoing health struggle. I have little time for extra activities. I haven't had much experience with kids. I'm not good at sales. I'm not very creative.

1.

2.

3.

4.

5.

Think of an experience when you learned the hard way that you had gone too far. What lesson(s) did you learn from that?

Example:

• When I worked seventy-hour weeks for two years and burned out, I learned I need a better work/life balance.

Name something in your life that could use more balance.

Example:

• I'm not finding any time for physical exercise.

If you were to name one area of your life or leadership in which you need to set some boundaries, knowing that if you don't it could lead to destructive outcomes, what might that be?

Example:

• I need to learn to say "no" to a few more people when they ask me for my time and energy. I can't do everything and be everywhere.

ACTION STEPS

1. Make a list of activities and involvements you are currently treating as a primary focus, and others you are giving secondary importance in to. Consider whether the list suggests that you need to make adjustments.

Example:

• Primary focuses: work, coaching a team, working on physical exercise

- Secondary focuses: my marriage, family, healthy diet, sleep

1.

2.

3.

4.

5.

2. Seek the objective help of a wise friend or a counselor to help you determine how to regain balance in your life or achieve a greater balance in your team.

3. Consider whether there are ways that you need to establish limitations for yourself or your team in order to have a more effective future.

Example:

- I need to work less and recreate more.
- I need to spend less time with community involvements so I have more time for my kids.
- I need to stop thinking about things related to work by eight p.m. so I can get to sleep earlier.

eleven

KNOW YOUR FAMILY

"Tennis is just a game. Family is forever."
—Serena Williams, tennis champion

Leadership Lesson
Your family is an extension of you; and, therefore, a self-aware person will be continually working at being a family-aware person.

We now come to an aspect of self-awareness that may seem out of place in a discussion about understanding yourself. In an earlier chapter, we looked at the influence of the family in which you were raised, your family of origin, and the experiences you have had in those earlier formative years of your life. In this chapter, we will be speaking of your current family, specifically your spouse and children, or depending on your stage of life and marital status, perhaps only one or the other. In some cases, the reality of a "mixed" family, or even multiple families through multiple marriages, makes the discussion even more complex. For the discussion at hand, however, let's focus more specifically on those to whom you are currently married and/or children who are still largely under your parental influence and probably still in your home. (This is not to say that those children who no longer share your home are not still influencing your life, nor you theirs. However, the impact of those with whom you currently share your home and your daily life is so much greater than those with whom you may have only occasional or infrequent contact.)

So how does having a better understanding of your family fit into a discussion about self-awareness? It should not be a stretch to realize that you and your family are an extension of one another, and what effects one affects all. If you want to live well, and lead well, you will give a great amount of energy to, and a great effort to understanding, your family. Your relationship to them, and consequently their relationship to you, will have a great impact on your life outside the home. Naturally, understanding your spouse and/or children is a lifelong process, but how are you doing at this?

At the time of this writing, my wife, Diane, and I have been married thirty-eight years, and our four children are all young adults in their twenties and thirties. To say that I thoroughly understand them and have nothing more to learn about them personally, or how I can better relate to them, would be untrue and unrealistic. My wife and I are still learning to understand and appreciate things about one another after more than three decades together.

Equally amazing is to see my children growing as adults, manifesting their own unique qualities and talents. I am continually learning how to relate to them in ways that enhance our relationships and mature us as people. Those relationships have come at the cost of a lot of effort, prayer, love, communication, perseverance, and even a number of bumps and painful episodes along the way. But they are growing into incredibly rewarding and enjoyable relationships that are one of the greatest parts of my life. Those relationships have also made me a better person, and even a better leader, because of what I have learned through those relationships. The same is true of my marriage. I am a different and better person and a more effective leader because of what I have learned through being a husband to my wife.

Whether your marriage experience has been long-lasting and rewarding, or short-lived and painful, and whether or not your experience as a parent mirrors mine, your experiences with your family have played a large role in making you the person you are today and the leader you are to others. Even those experiences you may consider negative have had an impact, for better or perhaps worse, on your development and formation as a person. The impact of your family relationships will either enhance or stunt your potential. Therefore, it is important to understand how you have been positively formed by those experiences or how they may have affected you in ways that can be self-sabotaging to the outcomes you desire in your life and in the lives of those you lead (including your family)!

Your life, like mine, has had a mixture of experiences that have affected you for better or for worse, and all have been opportunities for growth. For example, as I reflect on my parenting style, it represents an evolution that is ongoing. When my children were younger, and even into their early teens, I came to understand that my manner of directing or guiding them often tended to be authoritarian, even somewhat dictatorial. It was simpler (and in my mind more appealing) to give them commands and directives than to talk things through or try to come to a consensus.

It worked for a time, but after awhile I could recognize the mounting frustration in my children, as I realized I was denying them the opportunity to develop in their ability to be independent and make their own decisions. This, coupled with the fact that as teenagers they did not always respond well to directives and often did not want to listen to us as parents, brought me to re-examine and adapt my parenting style. As they continued growing into their teen years and young adulthood, those adjustments continued, depending on the individual nature of my children, their needs, and a growing sense of what would work best in parenting young adults. I have described our more recent parenting style as suggestive and supportive as opposed to directive. Amazingly, they have all responded well and we have been learning together how to relate to and influence each other.

It's important to mention that my parenting style often showed up in my leadership style, as well. This was especially true in the early years of our family. As a leader, I often acted individualistically, understanding little about teamwork, being rigid in my thinking, impatient when challenged, directive in style, and preferring to tell others what to do rather than help them to their own answers. Though I would never have thought of those I led as "children" and me as their "parent," my manner of leading could often be described with that image. As I have grown over the years as a person, as a parent, and as a spouse, many of those tendencies are no longer dominant, yet I am never far from defaulting to those former patterns. I have learned, however, that those tendencies do not describe healthy and effective family life, nor do they describe healthy and effective leadership.

What does it mean, then, to "know" your family? The answer could seem obvious, but I am not referring to knowing their name, hair color, favorite food, or pet peeve. I am also not referring to having a more informed general factual knowledge about them than those outside your home. No, I am speaking of an increasing awareness of deeper, more personal aspects of the way they think and live which reflect who they are at the deepest levels and which can influence their lives, and your relationship to them, in dynamic ways. In a very real sense, I am referring to having an understanding of those in your family that allows you to "read" them and understand what is behind their actions, responses, interactions, and transactions, and how that is affecting you and your relationship to them as a spouse or parent. As I indicated earlier, personality assessments can be a tremendous help in understanding those in your family. The more time you spend with them relating and communicating, the more you grow in your relationship to them and in your knowledge of their idiosyncrasies, way of thinking, and unique ways of revealing themselves as individuals.

If your marriage or relationship with your children is blossoming and increasing in strength and joy, you will carry over many of the principles you used in developing that relationship into your work environment, and the satisfaction and joy of those relationships will enhance what you do outside the home. On the other hand, if your relationships at home are a battleground, more a pain than a joy, and disunity or dysfunction seem to prevail, don't be quick to dismiss it as normal in a marriage or normal for child-parent relationships. These tensions may reveal deeper-rooted issues, which are abnormal and need to be addressed, not only for the sake of having a close-knit family, but also to avoid carrying unhealthy practices or unhealthy emotions into your roles outside the home. Getting to know your family involves, in part, some of the themes we considered earlier. As you understand more about your spouse's background influences, or your spouse's and children's' strengths, weaknesses, personalities, temperaments, personal passions, contextual influences, spiritual struggles or journeys, and limitations, you will be more adept at reading them and leading them in ways that are to their benefit and yours.

Your personal experience, your leadership effectiveness, and your family life are intertwined and immeasurably connected. How are you doing at growing into a self-aware, family-aware individual? It takes daily effort, lifelong commitment, and continual focus. But the results are worth it!

For Individual Consideration or Group Discussion

What are several words you would use to describe the current state of your family relationships (i.e., marriage, children)?

Example:

- Growing, strained, struggling, tense, rewarding, connected, unemotional

Name at least one way that you are better able to understand your spouse or children and read their words and actions than you were a year ago

Example:

- I now understand that when my son avoids me, it's because he is struggling with something that he feels embarrassed to talk to me about.
- I have learned that when my wife grows nontalkative with me, she is upset and I need to sensitively find out why she is struggling.

Are there situations at home that may be affecting you at work, or situations at work that may be affecting you at home? List as many possibilities as you can think of.

Example:

- At work: I've been working long hours. Could that be contributing to a less romantic feeling toward my wife and less time we've spent recently having fun together?
- At home: I'm having trouble relating to my kids and there's a lot of tension between us. Could that be a reason I've been more impatient with my team at work?

ACTION STEPS

1. Consider ways to build your relationship to your spouse and children in the next month, two months, three months.
2. Consider what adjustments might be necessary in your work (or involvements outside home) if it meant being able to strengthen your family relationships.

twelve

KNOW YOUR BODY

"Our bodies are apt to be our autobiographies."
—Frank Gelett Burgess, author

Leadership Lesson
How you treat your body will play a central role in the quality of how you live and how you influence others.

Most of us would rather forget about our body than study and know it. We over indulge it with rich and fattening (though tasty) foods and then lament the splurges, or at least the extra pounds they add. We adjust by buying larger clothing, or we diet to try to lose the weight we've gained. And who among us hasn't had the experience of trying with all our might to stick with the diet, only to find those stubborn pounds remaining, or once we've lost them, to find them returning all too easily!

We jog, walk, join Pilates or Zumba classes, invest in treadmills and other equipment for our homes, purchase gym memberships (and often talk about them more than actually use them), take weight loss pills, and engage in a multitude of other activities that at best represent a desire to be healthy, but all too often reflect a dissatisfaction toward our bodies. We cover parts of it with makeup, possibly to enhance what's there, but often to hide it. We look at the bodies of others on magazine covers and wish they were our own. Many go so far as to have it altered by plastic surgeries. We consume much of our time, resources, and energies feeding, bathing, caring for, improving, or altering our bodies.

Given the obsession we have with our physical bodies, it becomes a challenging task to say much that hasn't already been said or to wrap your mind around anything new concerning the knowledge of your body. However, the fact is that many of us either know our bodies little, or we act as though that's true. There are many things about the body that are impossible or impractical for you to know, and which you leave to professionals, such as your doctor, dentist, or other health practitioners. My chiropractor knows more about my structural parts than I ever will, but that's fine as long as he knows what he's doing and I feel better after he has reorganized me.

In developing a healthy self-understanding, it would be an enormous mistake to miss reminding you of the importance of your physical body to your overall health, effectiveness, and satisfaction in the way you live and to the impact you have on others. Like most of us, you may at least realize the importance of a balanced diet, regular exercise, rest, and daily basic vitamin supplements. You know that when your body feels worn out and tired, it's telling you of the need for rest. Even pain is an invaluable messenger, telling you that something is dangerously abnormal. No one likes pain, but how thankful you can be when it warns you of impending disaster and the need for attention or intervention!

The issue may not be one of knowing your body, but of not listening to it when you should. All of us, including you, have experienced periods of stress or physical challenge, perhaps due to deadlines at work, busy family schedules, or responsibilities that demand all you have physically, mentally, or emotionally. This is normal. What is abnormal is when these episodes become patterns and long-term practices, pushing you constantly to the limits of your being and taking a serious toll on your health, your relationships, or your ability to carry out your responsibilities. Perhaps at times you have acted without realizing the potential consequences, or you have come to a fork in the road of decision and chosen the wrong path.

Sometimes you need the knowledge and discernment of a professional to help you understand what's going on in your body and what actions are needed. Certainly you should attempt to have periodic preventative medical checkups if at all possible. I'm not a nutritional specialist, nor is this a health book, and so I will not go into details. However, it is obvious you also need to know enough about basic nutritional needs, eating practices, the benefits of exercise, the value of rest, the importance of balance and healthy rhythms in life, and the effects of abusing the body so that you can engage in self-care practices that benefit yourself and, as a result, those you influence. But wait! Knowing these things is not enough. They do you no good unless you do them! Reading these words may elicit feelings of guilt for knowing what is important but not having done it. We have all been there and done that.

The purpose of reminding you of this important aspect of self-awareness is not to paralyze you with guilt, but to mobilize you to action! We've all broken diets. We've all started exercise programs and given up. We've all put on weight through lack of disciplined eating. We've all deprived ourselves of the rest needed to get us through days of demanding responsibilities and busy activities. Nonetheless, it's not necessary for you, or any of us, to continue bad patterns or making poor choices. You can start fresh, you can change the way you think, you can stop thinking about momentary struggles and temporary fixes, and start thinking about the big picture and about long-term lifestyle choices that will be to your benefit and therefore the benefit of those around you.

Giving attention to your body is about more than quick fixes. It is also about quality of life and the ability to perform at your best in your relationships with others, remembering that the state of your own being will either affect them positively and constructively or negatively and perhaps destructively. Your health and well-being will affect the quality and potential of the way you think, the way you engage others, the mood and motivation of teams you lead, and the tone of your family life. It will impact the way you feel about yourself and the manner in which you present yourself to others.

While this discussion about the body has largely centered on general principles and universal applications, a word should also be said about the importance of knowing the individual, unique idiosyncrasies that may characterize you physically. There are characteristics, capacities, and needs that are unique to yourself and would not necessarily be true of those, for instance, in your spouse or the people at work. It may be due to something as obvious as age, longstanding health issues, or different metabolisms.

I have met some highly energetic people who seem to be able to accomplish much on little sleep, or at a quicker pace with seemingly less effort than me, and I have to admit envying them at times. The fact is, the difference between them and me is more than one of age or personality, but a different body metabolism.

I have a friend and peer in my organization who is involved in more activities and groups inside and outside the organization than anyone I've ever known. None of these are frivolous (all these activities seem to serve others in a variety of ways), and so he cannot be accused of "wasting his time." I often wonder when he sleeps, or how he manages on the minimal sleep he gets! On top of that, he drinks coffee like water, anytime of day or night. One's first response might be to think that's the secret: he's on a constant caffeine high! While he may be helped by caffeine to some measure, I think he simply enjoys coffee, and has a different metabolism than I do.

Admittedly, people like my friend with high metabolism and who tend to be highly involved and highly committed, need as much as you and I do to know their body and to put boundaries, safeguards, and practices into place that will prevent burnout and promote well-being. Yet it can be easy in the rush of activities and the crush of responsibilities to ignore your body when it starts "speaking" to you and warning of impending problems.

It's important to recognize the uniqueness and individuality of your own body from those of others. Your body is the only one you have to work with, and to try to live identically to those whose bodies have different needs, capacities, and characteristics than your own is to steer yourself toward troubled waters. On the other hand, it's only wise to recognize your physical realities and live accordingly, making adjustments if necessary, honoring your limitations, practicing sound principles within your unique physical makeup, and "listening" when your body is telling you that you're doing something beyond your reasonable limit or something that is producing a painful or unhealthy result. Not only that, but it's critical to leading a healthy and sustainable life, enjoying healthy relationships, and functioning at your optimum. Your body is vital to all you are and all you do. Steward it well, and it will serve you well!

For Individual Consideration or Group Discussion

List words describing your current state physically and what may be influencing that?

Example:

- Worn out → lack of sleep
- Strong, healthy → regular physical exercise
- Overweight → poor eating habits

1.

2.

3.

4.

5.

If you were to "listen" to your body, what might it be telling you?

Example:

- It's telling me to slow down the pace of my life.
- It's saying to me I can't keep up this level of stress for long.
- It's telling me I'm doing the right things for my health and need to continue.

What physical adjustments can you make that could improve the quality of your life and, therefore, your ability to influence others effectively?

Example:

• Regular exercise, balanced diet, longer sleep at night

ACTION STEPS

1. Join an exercise class or take out a gym membership and set up exercise times on your calendar as appointments you will keep. Consider hiring a personal trainer. Remember, too, it takes several weeks to establish a pattern, and only a short time to break one.

2. Have a full physical checkup and ask your doctor for ideas as to how to address any needs or concerns arising from that checkup.

3. Work with a nutritional expert to chart a plan for adjusting your eating habits in order to be healthier. This is not simply a diet, but a change in thinking, carrying you forward.

4. Establish an earlier time to get into bed, and do whatever will relax you in order to get to sleep (e.g., turn off the television, read, do a crossword puzzle or Sudoku).

thirteen

KNOW YOUR MENTAL HEALTH

"We are what we believe we are."
—C.S. Lewis, author

Leadership Lesson

Your mental state of being at any given time can be influenced by a wide variety of possibilities, affecting how you live and lead. Being aware of influences on your mental health can be preventative and life-giving by helping you read the warning signals, as well as in responding appropriately.

In the words of the song "State of Mind" on the album *Zoom* by the Electric Light Orchestra, life boils down to a changing mental state:

I was thinkin' of the past / I was tryin' to wrack my brain / I was lookin' at the future / I was tryin' to play the game / Didn't want to do it because I knew what I'd find / you're really only livin' in a state of mind /

Sometimes you get lost / sometimes you get found / in a state of mind / sometimes you're too high / sometimes you're too down / it's just a state of mind / Didn't want to do it cause I knew what I'd find / you're really only livin' in a state of mind

One of the reasons we enjoy listening to music is that it often expresses experiences in a way with which we can identify. I'll often be listening to songs of the 1960s and 1970s (pardon my vintage), and the song on the radio will immediately cause me to flash back to a time, an experience, or an emotion that I can somehow associate with that particular tune.

It can be enjoyable or sad for me when this happens, and it's easy to understand what's going on inside me as the song stirs a memory of the past. Many life experiences are not so obvious, however, and will leave you wondering why you are struggling or why your reality is what it is. Sometimes you can figure that out on your own, but at other times you need outside intervention or assistance. My vocation is not within the professional mental health field, but I offer here a few practical thoughts that can be helpful in recognizing your state of mind.

I was visiting some time ago with one of my organizational peers, and in the course of the conversation, I asked him how he was doing. He admitted that the past month had been a struggle, largely because he suffers from Seasonal Affective Disorder (SAD). SAD affects many people in our society, and some, like my friend, have discovered the source of their struggle and how to counter it. Many others struggle on, failing to understand that their struggle is caused by something abnormal for the body that needs specific treatment. For many, that treatment involves use of fluorescent "light boxes" for limited periods each day, in effect mimicking the effect of sunlight on their systems. My friend shared that he makes periodic visits to a tanning bed, which has the same effect, and while it hasn't cured him, it has made the disorder manageable.

Some sources suggest up to 25 percent of our North American population struggles with SAD. Its cause appears to be the effect on brain chemicals when deprived of light or sunshine, which produces symptoms, such as sadness, depression, irritability, headaches, or sleep disruption. Thankfully, my friend understands this, and is not only living a normal life, but is leading others effectively, even when facing a difficult seasonal challenge each year.

Having a strong and healthy self-awareness requires that you have a reasonable understanding of your current state of mental health. The previous chapter regarding physical health, and the discussion at hand regarding mental health, are equally important and undeniably related. There are differences between the two, yet there are mutually impacting connections, as well. Take for instance those who have done little to maintain their physical health, and as a result may feel worse and worse about themselves, continuing a downward spiral into depression, anxiety, unhappiness, or other self-destructive emotions.

At times understanding and responding to your physical health may be easier than understanding your mental health because the former can be easily recognizable or observable, at least by the trained physician if not also yourself. Often, your mental state of being can be just as easily recognized through your emotions or actions. At other times, however, your mental health deals with issues that are unseen and are often difficult to diagnose by the untrained individual. It's a great challenge to look beyond the readily observable to identify something invisible to the eye or deep within a person's spirit. Mental health experts can be of great help. However, you don't have to possess a Ph.D. in psychology, nor do you need a wealth of knowledge, to be able to have a basic grasp of your mental state at any given moment. You will need to be honest with yourself though and be willing to do some self-assessment.

There are many ways to describe mental health, but I would offer seven unofficial, but hopefully helpful, descriptors in your mental health spectrum. These represent various states that the average person may experience, recognizing you can fluctuate between these (and experience them) to various degrees. On a scale of 1 (best state) to 7 (lowest state), those descriptors are: 1) elation; 2) congruence; 3) relative serenity; 4) stressed and pressed; 5) worn out; 6) burned out; and 7) desperate or depressed.

Elation represents those periods of time when your life has plenty of reasons to feel good and few to upset you. These periods do not last indefinitely but they are a welcome oasis in your life journey. You feel great pleasure and in great spirits about your life. While you know these feelings won't always fill your life, these periods of elation are renewing and exciting. They are what some would refer to as the "mountaintop" times versus more difficult times in the "valley."

Congruence represents that state of mind in which you find fulfillment in your identity, compatibility between your mental and physical state (and may I suggest your spiritual self?), and an overall acceptance and satisfaction with your direction in life. You aren't living on the highs of the "mountaintop," but you are more focused on the positive elements of your life than the negative ones. You feel accepting of your real self and are pleased at seeing that real self growing and changing for the better, even in the midst of difficulties and concerns.

Relative serenity can depend on the person and situation. But generally speaking, it represents a sense of peacefulness in the midst of change, difficulty, or challenge. It's not a place of excitement or elation, but of feeling calm inside when there are ample reasons not to be. Relative serenity represents a lesser state of satisfaction and contentment than congruence, not necessarily seeing your present realities as those you would like to experience permanently, while yet having a strong sense inwardly that you are okay and your circumstances will work out.

Stressed and pressed represents more than your experience for a few passing minutes, but for a period of time when the pressures of life, job, family, finances, health, or other factors, singularly or in combination, cause you to feel like you are carrying a mental weight around. That weight may lead to anxiety, fear, frustration, or a variety of other emotions.

Worn out is something we all feel quite commonly, either in a physical, mental, or emotional sense, and the causes could be many. Perhaps you've pushed hard for a period of time without enough rest, or you've lost balance and overworked yourself. It may have left you feeling depleted with much less energy. Being worn out can happen sporadically, or it can become a more regular state of being. If not remedied, it can lead to lethargic living, or even worse, burn out.

To **burn out** in the true sense of the word means you cross a line, which leads to a serious mental health issue, in a sense a mental illness, and which deeply impacts you, threatening your well-being. The causes can be numerous, including suppressed anger, and the symptoms can include such things as:

- Low to no motivation
- Cynicism
- Pessimism
- Lethargy
- Fatigue despite receiving adequate rest
- Withdrawal from relationships

- Critical attitude
- Hopelessness
- Inability to function at a normal level

If you are truly "burned out" and not just "worn out," full recovery may take a long time, and you will certainly need the help and support of others, including that of professionals, such as a doctor or counselor.

This is also true of a seventh state of mental health I have included. While not the sole cause of this, the effects of "burn out," for example, if not dealt with, can become one of the causes leading to an even more serious state of feeling, which I've labeled **desperate or depressed**. There most certainly are lesser degrees of desperation and depression that can be part of your experience. However, I am speaking here of deep internal struggle that produces an ongoing sense of feeling extremely low, or at worst, thoughts of ending it all. This state, too, will most certainly need the assistance of others, such as a counselor, clergy, or professional mental health expert. When you are in its grips, you are not yourself and can make illogical, unwise decisions or take unhealthy actions.

Since I am not a mental health professional, I would not pretend to be offering standard clinical labels. However, I have experienced most of these described states personally, have observed all of them in many others, and have studied them enough to be able to find meaning and a strong dose of reality in this simple seven-stage spectrum. Having at least a basic grasp of the general states in which you can find yourself, and being willing to allow those with more knowledge to help diagnose your struggles, or being willing to listen not only to them but to what you may be sensing inwardly, will be critical in continuing your forward progress in learning to live and lead more effectively.

So how would you describe your current state of mind, and what might be influencing you?

Wherever you would place yourself on the spectrum, a simple and obvious reminder of some of the influences on your mental health may be helpful. A number of these will influence your sense of well-being and are probably more obvious, yet others may not be quite so obvious. The following list is by no means exclusive, but represents what I believe can be some of the most common challenges to your mental well-being. As you read the list, ask yourself how you would rate these factors in describing you on a scale of 1 (strongly describes you) to 5 (does not describe you). Be aware they are not listed in any order of priority or significance.

Which of these may be influencing your current state of mind and mental health?

1. **Expectations:** This may include expectations you have of yourself or that others have of you. These expectations may be realistic and achievable or unrealistic and discouraging. Score _____

2. **Workaholic tendencies:** Work regularly absorbs most of your time and energies. Work drives you, and everything else in your life is secondary. Score _____

3. **Abuse of good boundaries:** You have a hard time saying no or setting healthy boundaries. You struggle to respect yourself by being disciplined in working at balance. Score _____

4. **Season of life or of year:** The time of year or the stage of your life has different implications for you. Score _____

5. **Long-term high output:** Over the years you have pushed hard; intensity and stress have tended to outweigh efforts at renewal and replenishing.

Imbalanced living, minimal ongoing learning, or weak priorities may also contribute to feeling like a well that has run dry. Score _____

6. **Bodily chemical dysfunction:** (This needs the diagnosis of professionals to determine.) You seem to continually function at a low level or at a minimum. Score _____

7. **Addiction or addictive tendencies:** Addiction to something that becomes the driving force of your life is more obvious. Less obvious may be addictive tendencies and patterns which you may want to deny, but cannot if being completely honest. Among many things fueling addictive tendencies may be a sense of entitlement, a need to escape, narcissism, poor self-image. Score _____

8. **Relational dysfunction:** This can include guilt over something in the past, unresolved conflicts, or unforgiveness, which creates internal or relational turmoil. Score _____

9. **The normal rhythms and responsibilities of life:** Life is a challenge in numerous ways. Every person in every stage of life faces challenges considered normal.Score _____

10. **Poor fit:** Your current situation is a poor fit for your personality, skills, or the things you are passionate about. Your difficulty with change in a constantly changing environment, the mismatch of your abilities and strengths to your job role, etc., create turmoil. Score _____

11. **A sense of loss of control and hopelessness:** Major factors in your life seem out of control, and as a result, you find yourself feeling significant hopelessness or stress. Score _____

12. **Cultural norms:** Norms can be abnormal and manipulating, such as North American culture's equating business with success and self-worth, which is false and leads to dysfunctional thinking. Score _____

13. **Unwillingness to admit or deal with our limitations:** We all have limitations and areas of strengths and weaknesses. Yet, trying to be what you're not or to be like someone else, or failure to admit and live within your limitations, pushes you unhealthy directions. Score _____

14. **Resistance to change:** Different from being an issue of poor fit, you tend to resist change instead of recognizing that change is quite normal and can be a positive opportunity for you or your organization, or that leadership is often about discerning needed changes, then motivating and helping others to process that. Score _____

15. **Lack of accountability in friendships or other relationships:** Lacking people who can speak into your life freely and honestly can lead to unhealthy practices. Score _____

16. **Individualism:** Individualists easily move beyond healthy boundaries by carrying too much themselves or being too proud to ask for help, convincing themselves they can do it better than anyone else and are irreplaceable. Score _____

17. **Dissatisfaction with your physical appearance and realities:** More than wanting good, healthy practices in exercise and eating, personal dissatisfaction or unwillingness to accept realities about your physical being or what you can or cannot do can weigh heavily and even become consuming. Score _____

18. **Gender-specific factors:** Inequities or practices and attitudes in the workplace or elsewhere create mental or emotional stress for you. Score _____

19. **Worry:** While personality and mental disorders* can tend to influence this, excessive or regular worry can be wearing, especially when worrying over high priorities, such as family, finances, or the

necessities of life. Score_____ *Note: *Mental disorders which have been professionally diagnosed, such as anxiety disorders, severe depression, bipolar disorder, schizophrenia, or others need to be treated and addressed with as much urgency as any physical problem.*

20. **Laughter deficit:** Laughter is one of the greatest medicines of daily life*, but if life lacks laughter, one of the greatest sources of health and healing is missing. Score _____

    *Note: *"Laughter reduces tension, massages the heart, stimulates blood circulation, increases the body's natural painkillers, reduces stress, and helps the lungs breathe easier . . . [it] enhances relationships and is a key ingredient for a more satisfying marriage."*[1]

21. **Ability to keep the big picture:** Daily demands, pressures, and stresses can drive you to become narrowly focused and diminished in motivation. You may feel like you're left slugging it out daily and focused more on self-preservation than the big picture or an all-encompassing perspective. Score _____

For Individual Consideration or Group Discussion

How would you describe your mental state of health, using the seven suggested descriptors? Why? Be specific.

1. Elation:

2. Congruence:

3. Relative serenity:

4. Stressed and pressed:

5. Worn out:

1. Tim Wright and Lori Woods, *The Ministry Marathon: Caring for Yourself While You Care for the People of God*, (Nashville: Abingdon Press, 1999), 82–83.

6. Burned out:

7. Desperate or depressed:

As you read through the list of factors that can influence your mental state of health, which ones did you score lowest in (4s or 5s), and which ones might you need the assistance of a professional to determine whether there are any issues in particular to be concerned about?

Example:

- Bodily chemical function → I am tired all the time despite lots of sleep.
- Relational dysfunction → I seem to be unable to form close relationships.

Which of those factors on the list that you identified as applying to you are you or are you not able to change or control?

Example:

- Expectations → I can control my own, but not those of others.
- Season of life → I can't change that, but I can control how I respond to it.

ACTION STEPS

1. Consider the factors on the influencers list in which you scored low (4s or 5s) and whether they represent something you can begin to address, and how.

2. See a specialist to explore potential solutions to a perceived problem.

    Example:

-   Financial stresses → financial counselor
-   Depression, burnout → physician, psychologist, counselor, therapist
-   Family stresses → family counselor or local clergy
-   Constant anxiety, fear → counselor or psychologist
-   Overworked, tired → employer or supervisor; time management coach
-   Desperation → a close friend, counselor, psychologist
-   Addiction → addictions counselor, specialized organization for addictive tendencies
-   Poor fit at job → job supervisor, human resources/job counselor

3. Schedule a vacation soon.

4. Read resources to help you better understand areas of interest concerning mental health. A professional counselor or mental health specialist could be contacted for suggested materials or books, and so could your local library.

fourteen

KNOW YOUR DREAM SCHEME

"When you have a sense of your own identity and a vision of where you want to go in your life, then you have a basis for reaching out to the world and going after your dreams for a better life."
—*Stedman Graham, author of You Can Make It Happen*

Leadership Lesson
Knowing and pursuing dreams not only can enhance your own life, but it can be a means of leading others and impacting their lives, too, as they observe what you model, or work with you in pursuing something yet to be realized in the future.

On a television episode of *America's Funniest Videos*, a prize-winning segment portrayed a kindergarten "graduating" class. As part of the ceremony, each child was asked, "What do you want to be when you grow up?" The responses included "a vampire bat." But the one that won the prize was a little boy whose response was "I don't want to grow up!"

What a great response!

All of us can remember being asked that question at some point in our lives, and perhaps you responded with an answer preconditioned by your early life exposure to certain jobs that seemed appealing, or at least paid well. I have jokingly said to others, "I never grew up; I just got older!" That statement, unfortunately, is all too true of many people. Others, however, have had a different experience. A few people knew from early in life what they were destined to do as an occupation. Most of us, though, have engaged in trial and error throughout our lives, eliminating some possibilities and contemplating others, until at some point we either pursued our chosen occupation or took a job that could support us until we could find something better or figure out what we want to do "when we grow up."

Having desired outcomes for the future, or what I've called a "dream scheme," is an important aspect of self-awareness because it relates to what motivates you. This is a different aspect than your personal passions (Chapter 7), although very related. Knowing your passions may help you identify what inwardly compels you and yearns for expression, but is that motivating you *toward* something? Passions tend to become chief motivators in your life and drive you to dream about possibilities. However, if that compelling passion and inner desire do not find expression in pursuit of a dream, a tangible result, then that passion may turn to frustration, disappointment, and even anger because you feel short changed in life. Dreams motivate you toward something and give you hope and purpose.

What are you dreaming about these days? Is it an expression of a passion, and is it realistic? By realistic, I do not mean easily achievable, as many dreams take much time, sacrifice, and effort to achieve. However, some of us tend to have dreams that are so far beyond reasonable that our expectations may have lost touch with reality.

Dreams drive you to pursue things that do not presently exist but you believe could happen in the future, and they often involve a process that forms and shapes you as you stretch and work toward those dreams. Even if those dreams are never achieved, the process can make you a better person (and a better leader) for having endured it and pursued it.

Dreams are people shapers and world shakers! They tend to make the future better for you, and hopefully others as well. In fact, what greater purpose can leadership serve than making the future better for others in some way, and perhaps in the process better for yourself? Are you dreaming about ways the future could be better for you, your family, and your organization, and what are you doing tangibly to pursue those dreams?

Having a dream scheme is also different from simply knowing your stage of life (Chapter 1). Understanding what drives and motivates you in that life stage is one thing, but letting that motivate you toward tangible outcomes and being intentional about reaching those outcomes is an important next step and expression of understanding your life stage. For myself, my twenties and thirties were a time of having some pretty impressive, and even unrealistic dreams, but the dreams of my youthfulness were motivating. However, as I moved further into my thirties and forties, the busy demands of raising a family, firming up a career pathway, and trying to meet the many needs of a family, as well as my own (along with the process of maturing and learning to better discern between what might or might not ever be realistically possible) led to revised, or even abandoned, dreams. In fact, demands often took precedence over dreams. Yet some of those dreams needed to be revised or abandoned as my understanding of myself and the best pathways for my life grew and gave birth to new dreams.

In my fifties, I became reinvigorated with dreams for the future and am still excited about pursuing them. I hope I never stop dreaming about possibilities and pursuing them, even as I move into the later years of my life, because to be without dreams is to be condemned to an unmotivating existence and a hollow sense of life! It is also true that to have dreams that only serve yourself, and are not about making things somehow better for others, can be equally hollow because there's a desire in all of us to make an impact and difference in life, as well as to love and be loved. What characterizes love more than a desire to consider others' needs or interests, even at the occasional expense of your own? Dreaming of ways you can use your influence (leadership) for making a difference in others' lives and this world is the greatest possible application of leadership.

History abounds with examples of people who impacted others by pursuing their dreams. Amelia Earhart was motivated to fly. She had attempted studies in medicine and a variety of jobs, including social work, but after riding in an airplane with her father while attending an air show, she was hooked on flying. If you know about Amelia, you know this led to a string of events involving her as an aviator, including a cross-Atlantic solo flight in 1932, the first solo flight from Hawaii to the North American mainland in 1935, as well as speed records between Los Angeles and Mexico City and between Mexico City and New York that same year.

In 1937, Earhart made her ill-fated attempt to fly around the world, and while flying over the Pacific, she disappeared along with her navigator into the pages of history. One of her driving desires had been to accomplish something that would be useful in this world. At one point she made the following statement: "My ambition is to have this wonderful gift produce practical results for the future of commercial flying and for the women who may want to fly tomorrow's planes."[1]

Her influence has inspired many women to follow suit, opening the field of aviation much wider to women than had ever been the case prior to Amelia pursuing her dreams. A prime example is the participation and leadership of women aviators in the US space program, such as astronauts Sally Ride (first female American in space), Roberta Bondar (first female Canadian in space), Mae Jemison (first female African American in space), Eileen Collins (first female to command and pilot a shuttle), Pamela Melroy (second female to command a shuttle), and dozens of other female astronauts from a variety of nations. While there is no way to know the degree of Amelia Earhart's personal influence on these women, it's likely that Amelia, and others who followed, served as inspirations and leaders to these people, as well as numerous others, in pursuing their own dreams to make things better, whether in aviation or other fields of influence.

What if Amelia Earhart had never tuned into her inner motivations, had never taken a flying lesson, and had settled into a more traditional role for a woman of her time? What if she had opted for something less difficult and more common? It would be difficult to say whether so many female aviators would have followed, but it could probably be said with certainty that because of this courageous pioneer who pursued her dream, many others were encouraged to also pursue theirs.

Playwright, poet, and novelist Miguel de Cervantes wrote, "Love not what you are, but only what you may become." *Dreams call passions into action. Passions turned into action make a difference.*

Are you listening to your inner motivations? Are you taking steps toward seeing your passions launched into producing tangible results? Is

---

1. Amelia Earhart, available at *http://womenshistory.about.com/od/quotes/a/amelia_earhart.htm.*

there something within you that's been yearning for expression and has you occasionally thinking "What if . . .?" Self-awareness calls for you to know the dreams locked inside you and find ways for those dreams to become reality!

For Individual Consideration or Group Discussion

If you could imagine a picture that would describe your future, personally and vocationally, what would be some of the elements or images included in that picture? List them below.

Example:

- A dollar sign representing freedom from debt and the ability to be generous to others
- A globe representing my desire to travel
- Children representing a desire for family
- Wedding rings representing a strong and happy marriage
- A diploma representing graduation with a degree
- Jogging representing good health and regular exercise

What are one or two ideas or possibilities that excite you as you think about the future in terms of your personal or family life, or your job, and are they achievable?

Example:

- Owning my own business → yes, achievable
- Taking a space flight → possible, but not likely at my age
- My kids graduating from a college → yes, achievable
- Becoming a supervisor at work → yes, achievable
- Adopting a child → yes, achievable

List tangible steps you could begin taking toward your dream(s).

Example:

- Adopting a child → contact an adoption agency; pray; financially plan
- College degrees for my kids → begin a savings account for their future
- Owning my own business → take business courses; develop my expertise; develop a business plan

ACTION STEPS

1. Talk to someone you know who has been successful at creating a tangible result in an area of your interest and dreams.

2. Read biographies about people who achieved results you dream about.

3. Make a list of three things you will do, or start, within one week to take tangible steps toward a personal dream.

4. Discuss your dream with your spouse in order to seek support and explore it further together.

5. Identify the greatest obstacle to achieving your dream, and then make a list of ways to potentially address that obstacle.

6. Develop a two- to five-year timeline for pursuing your dream and attach specific time-related goals to it.

7. Consider the motivations behind your dream and whether pursuing that dream would be primarily to make a positive impact in others' lives or to achieve primarily selfish purposes. Remember, dreams can bring a measure of personal satisfaction, but the greatest satisfaction will come by making a difference in the lives of others.

fifteen

KNOW YOUR BLIND SPOTS

"I have come to believe that there is a deeper person in many of us who is not unlike an assassin. This deeper person can be the source of attitudes and behaviors we normally stand against in our conscious being. But it seeks to destroy us and masses energies that—unrestrained—tempt us to do the very things we 'believe against'."
—*Gordon MacDonald, author of When Leaders Implode*

Leadership Lesson
Personal blind spots will have potentially damaging and destructive effects in your life and leadership role(s). Therefore, it is important to be learning how to identify and avoid those personal minefields.

Like many others, you may have had the experience of receiving an email notice that your credit card information has been compromised and you need to take steps to confirm or provide certain personal information to correct the problem. The real problem is that it was another attempt to scam you, as with a multitude of other consumers, into providing information that will allow the party at the other end to steal your identity, funds, and peace of mind. I'm sure you have received many of these, as I have, and perhaps have been tempted momentarily to respond, before coming to your senses. It may even be that your alertness in such situations has come at the expense of having fallen for such an approach, even just once. Yet once was enough to make you reluctant to ever again provide personal information to unknown entities over the telephone or the computer.

Another popular scam which comes in a variety of forms, and frequently shows up on your computer, is an invitation from someone, typically overseas, to help them process a large amount of funds for which they will pay you generously out of those funds for your assistance. It usually involves providing information or sending money, which supposedly sets in motion an offer that classically is "too good to be true." The variations are numerous, but the common factor in all of them is an unknown party who is counting on your greed, gullibility, or ignorance to participate in an offer of a lifetime. As you received these offers, perhaps you have shaken your head and muttered under your breath "What kind of idiot do they think I am?"

Sadly, there are many people who fall for these scams and schemes and lose thousands, even tens of thousands, of dollars to these unscrupulous sources who are social predators. Many of those who have been duped are mentally intelligent and experienced in life. When the experience of being cheated and robbed is past, they understandably feel foolish, embarrassed, and upset at having allowed themselves to fall for what should have been obvious, or at least should have been held in check by common sense. However, they fell prey to a personal "blind spot." Their gullibility was greater than they realized, or the level of greed that drove them to let down their guard was deeper than they would have thought. Perhaps their motivation to help another person shaded their ability to read obvious signals or recognize red flags. In some way, a personal shortcoming or weakness overwhelmed what they would have normally thought characterized them. They may have even been aware of their tendency or temptation to be led off the desired pathway, but they'd either misjudged that tendency or ignored it. "Blind spots" leave you susceptible and vulnerable.

I do not write as one who is a stranger to blind spots. We all have them. Are you learning what yours are? Sometimes a hard experience is your best teacher. In other situations, awareness may come through the honest comments and helpful observations of others. I recall one experience flowing from the most difficult period of our marriage, which was the result of my accepting the leadership role in which I serve at the time of this writing.

At the time, we lived in a small city in the northern part of British Columbia, having moved there from the Vancouver area. My new role would now call for us to move back to the Vancouver area so that I could join the work of a district leadership team. The older home we had purchased and renovated in the north was comfortable and would not normally be a difficult home to sell. However, a number of newer homes had been constructed in the city as the local economy began to improve. Newer homes, complete with newer furnaces, better windows, and higher energy efficiency than our own and in a lower price bracket than ours, were springing up in significant numbers. I needed to join my new team within a short time frame, so I left and moved ahead of the family, thinking the process of selling our home would be taken care of quickly. Days became weeks, and weeks became months. On occasion, my wife and I would travel to be with one another, even if only for a weekend.

The struggle of being apart began to turn to an emotional distancing. Perhaps this was a survival mechanism. Eventually, though, I found myself in my director's office being told that this separation was detrimental to my marriage, and if I did not move my wife to my present location within a month, I may not have a job! My immediate inward reaction was to feel somewhat offended, as if I were a child being spoken to by a parent. After all, I was a mature adult, I knew my family and my limits (I thought), and I didn't need others telling me how to run my life or cope with a very challenging time. I valued my job, however, and after thanking my director for his concern, I left his office feeling a bit bothered, but also grateful for his honesty in observing and challenging something which he felt was growing increasingly dangerous for my relationship. I continued reflecting on his words in the days that followed, and after the initial defensiveness, I realized I had been caught up in a personal blind spot, thinking I could handle it, but not realizing, or at least admitting, how destructive the situation was becoming to our marriage. The difficulty of those months of separation was beginning to wear heavily on us, and we couldn't see it as well as others could in our determination to survive the separation. Yet, if it had gone on much longer, our family could have paid a more serious price.

Like each of us, you have patterns, tendencies, or characteristics that can potentially affect you in negative ways and blind you to potentially destructive outcomes. Early in my career, I recall having to learn that as hard as I worked and well-intentioned as I was, I was a poor delegator and tried to do too much myself. I have had to continually work to overcome that, not only for my own balance and effectiveness, but also in order not to rob others of the opportunity to grow and develop through personal involvement, and even by making mistakes. After all, it's often through our mistakes that we grow the most. However, pain, errors, and occasional failures are not something any of us want to experience, so I tried to minimize the possibility of these by doing as much as I could myself and trying to control the outcomes.

This was a blind spot for me as a developing leader. I felt I was doing what was best, what was most natural for me, yet it limited the potential of both me and others. Good leaders must breed other leaders, and this requires giving up some of the control and taking on the risk of failures in order to place confidence in others. This is a difficult, but valuable, lesson that many of us need to learn.

In earlier chapters, I mentioned a few potential blind spots, such as inner issues and unresolved tensions rooted in the experiences with one's family of origin, or in developing a sense of entitlement, or unhealthy sexual behaviours that can lead to addictive practices or relational breakdowns. Pride, ego, family problems, lack of rest, work overload, the tendency to procrastinate, poor dietary practices, and little exercise can also apply. So can repressed anger, fear of failure, the driving need to prove yourself, emotional instability, fear of change, effects of aging, chemical or hormonal body changes, loneliness, failure to understand your personality type or temperament, and a tendency to say "yes" too often. We could add to this list:

- Inadequate training
- Unwillingness to deal with conflict
- Feeling threatened by peers or teammates
- Failure to understand the culture of your organization or your surrounding community or those you serve

- Unwillingness to let go of tradition or routines
- Intergenerational ignorance
- Unhealthy willingness to compromise values
- Personal ambition
- Lust for power
- Unwillingness to forgive
- Prejudice

The list is not exhaustive, but it is impressive in realizing there may be a host of potential blind spots that can trigger unhealthy responses and undesirable effects.

How can you identify and guard against the potentially negative effects of personal blind spots? You may be able to identify at least one or two by meditating on the list above and by reflecting on some of the more difficult experiences you have had in your life and leadership. Put aside the temptation to rationalize and make excuses. Ask yourself very honestly how your own behaviour and decisions may have contributed and whether this may reveal a potential blind spot. You could also ask a trusted friend or someone close to you who knows you well whether they have observed any behaviors in you that could potentially lead to problems or derail you, whether on the list I mentioned or something else not included. Be humble and nondefensive, honestly seeking to address potentially harmful issues. This kind of self-reflection or observation by others can be a bit unsettling, but enormously helpful.

All of us realize, yet none of us likes to admit, that you can be your own worst enemy at times, and that you have elements of your life that can work against your dreams, goals, and best desires. Only by being honest with yourself, and allowing others to be honest with you, as well, will you find that what you may feel is momentarily uncomfortable or even painful can lead to a stronger life and greater impact on others. Self-honesty and humility require you to view yourself through lenses that may not be shaded to your liking, but your willingness to do so is worth it! It will lead to great dividends in your growth as an individual and your ability to make a real difference in the roles and relationships that are part of your present and future life!

For Individual Consideration or Group Discussion

List personal blind spots you are already aware of.

Example:

- Gullibility to the urgent requests I hear from sources via my email.
- I want to help others so much I can drive myself beyond healthy limits.
- I don't have good common sense, so I need others who do.
- I can overreact to any statements that threaten my self-esteem.

1.

2.

3.

4.

5.

Think about examples of situations where you have responded in unhealthy ways or made poor choices, and whether those may possibly represent a blind spot.

Example:

- At times when I've felt backed into a corner, I have said things I should not have.

- At times when my spouse has said things I've interpreted as critical, I have quickly gotten defensive and lashed out verbally.

- When I am put into situations for which I am untrained, I am afraid to ask for help.

List the name(s) of at least one or two people whom you would feel comfortable in giving freedom and permission to speak honestly to you if they observe unhealthy behaviours or have concerns about potential blind spots in your life.

ACTION STEPS

1. Ask your spouse, or a trusted friend, what their observation would be of blind spots that could be a source of potential problems for you.

2. Put safeguards in place to deal with potential blind spots.

   Example:

- To counter impulsiveness or gullibility in handling your money, agree with your spouse or a close friend to always run it by them before spending any amount over $50 on nonessential expenditures.

- Give freedom and permission to your team to draw attention to your tendency to overwork and live out of balance.

- To deal with a tendency toward procrastination, set your clock/watch ahead several minutes and plan to be at any appointment ten minutes early.

3. Identify potential blind spots that would create problems and hinder effectiveness for your team or those you lead.

   Example:

- Tendency to depend too much on one person's input

- Micromanaging details of their jobs rather than empowering them

- Lacking a sense of interdependent teamwork because we don't really know each other

EPILOGUE

You are a leader! You may not think of yourself as such, but you are, whether or not you may be in a paid leadership role. Each one of us influences and impacts others. Whether it's your family, your spouse, those in your neighbourhood, friends in the community, those in your organization, or others, you are an influence upon them, and leadership is primarily influencing others toward specific outcomes.

Your influence may be intentional or unintentional, but how you live, and the manner in which you relate to those around you, will directly or indirectly affect others. The question, then, is not so much whether you are a leader, but whether your leadership influence on others is positive or negative, constructive or destructive. Is your influence "pushing" them toward outcomes that will help or hinder them? Will it enhance or weaken them in their own development? Will the end result be that others' lives are better for you being in it, or will their lives be the same as if they had never known you?

For those of you who are in paid vocational roles of leadership, or who may be in unpaid appointed roles of influence within groups or organizations, the implications of this book are important, because how you lead them will either "push" them toward greater passion for (and participation in) the mission of your group, or it will lead to frustration and loss of motivation. The latter will, in turn, limit or even prevent your ability to realize your own goals and desires, not to mention those of your organization.

Being a self-aware individual is a great gift to yourself as well as to others because, in knowing yourself, you also come to better understand others. It allows you to make better choices and address damaging issues, to strengthen how you relate to others, and it creates potential for outcomes that fuel your excitement and passion. It doesn't deliver you from all life's challenges and struggles, but it does help you avoid a number of pitfalls, and helps minimize the chances of failing, burning out, or damaging yourself (or others) in ways that can impact for a long time, if not a lifetime. This enables you to keep moving forward instead of constantly taking two steps forward and three steps backward. It allows you to live in ways that are consistent with who you are and who you aren't. It allows you to keep imagining a better future, instead of becoming continually wallowed in the mud of past actions and decisions that could have been handled differently. It empowers you with an invaluable means of discernment.

Self-aware people become self-aware leaders, and self-aware leaders are well positioned to make a real difference in ways that are unique and exciting to them, not to mention rewarding to others. May the words of this book give you hope as you step into the future, and may your life be a gift that flavors the lives of others in ways that will make them grateful that your life intersected theirs! You are wonderfully and uniquely designed. May you more fully grasp this in the days to come!